"Increasingly, research is showing that dialectical behavior therapy (DBT) can be a useful treatment for a range of mental health problems. In *The Dialectical Behavior Therapy Skills Workbook for Anxiety*, Chapman, Gratz and Tull strip away the jargon and walk the reader step-by-step through this treatment, showing the reader how to apply DBT skills to anxiety. This workbook will provide many anxiety sufferers with much-needed relief."

—David F. Tolin, PhD, ABPP, director of the Anxiety Disorders Center at the Institute of Living and author of *Face your Fears*

"I strongly recommend this self-help book for people suffering from various forms of anxiety. These authors effectively describe in lay terms how mindfulness, distress tolerance, emotion regulation and interpersonal effectiveness skills augment the more traditional applications of cognitive behavioral therapy strategies in the treatment of anxiety. In this book, the reader will find clinical vignettes, diagrams, and useful worksheets in this book that enhance the process of learning of these DBT tools."

—Alec L. Miller, PsyD, professor of clinical psychiatry and behavioral sciences at Albert Einstein College of Medicine in Bronx, NY

"Symptoms of anxiety, worry, and panic are integral to the emotional disorders and respond to a core set of psychological interventions. In this outstanding workbook, the authors pull together some of the most creative and scientifically-proven procedures for managing out-of-control emotions, including anxiety. These dialectical behavior therapy skills should benefit everyone suffering the ravages of anxiety disorders."

—David Barlow, PhD, professor of psychology and psychiatry and founder and director emeritus of the Center for Anxiety and Related Disorders at Boston University

"A clear, practical guide that combines evidence-based approaches with rich clinical wisdom. Filled with innovative and practical advice as well as lively metaphors and engaging case examples, this book is sure to help readers struggling with anxiety find a balance between acceptance and change. I highly recommend this book and these authors."

—Lizabeth Roemer, PhD, coauthor of *The Mindful Way Through Anxiety*

"For many, the struggle to control anxiety can be an exhausting, consuming, and seemingly endless challenge. Fortunately, *The Dialectical Behavior Therapy Skills Workbook for Anxiety* offers a number of well researched, easy to implement strategies that can help readers to better understand, accept, and manage their anxiety, improve their relationships, and engage more fully in their lives."

—Susan M. Orsillo, PhD, psychology professor at Suffolk University

"This is an excellent application of dialectical behavior therapy (DBT) skills for people struggling with anxiety, panic attacks, and related problems. Not only will readers gain a better understanding of what these problems are, they'll also learn some very practical and effective skills to cope with them. Many thanks to the authors for bringing the success of DBT to people suffering with anxiety."

> —John Forsyth, PhD, director of the Anxiety Disorders Research Program at the University at Albany, SUNY and author of *The Mindfulness and Acceptance Workbook for Anxiety*

"To be relieved of anxiety is often a person's highest priority for therapy. This book allows access to the powerful DBT methods that that can provide that relief. It is not always possible to join a DBT skills training group, but it is possible to understand and use Marsha Linehan's transformative work by reading this practical interpretation."

> —Kate Northcott, MA, MFT, DBT therapist in private practice with Mindfulness Therapy Associates and director of New Perspectives Center for Counseling in San Francisco, CA

"Alexander Chapman and his colleagues have provided a much-needed, thorough resource in *The Dialectical Behavior Therapy Skills Workbook for Anxiety*. Offering DBT skills and emphasizing mindfulness practice, this book provides helpful information and practical worksheets, and will be a valuable tool for both people experiencing anxiety and the clinicians treating them."

> —Sheri Van Dijk, MSW, RSW, psychotherapist in Ontario, Canada, and coauthor of *The Dialectical Behavior Therapy Skills Workbook for Bipolar Disorder*

"*The Dialectical Behavior Therapy Skills Workbook for Anxiety* is a welcome new tool for anyone who is burdened with anxiety, or who works to help those who are. This is a clear, practical, and easy-to-use workbook. It holds the promise of increased understanding, real relief, and personal growth for anyone who is willing to take some time to read the text and apply themselves to the exercises."

> —Jeffrey Brantley, MD, DFAPA, founder and director of the mindfulness-based stress reduction program at Duke Integrative Medicine and author of *Calming Your Anxious Mind*

"*The Dialectical Behavior Therapy Skills Workbook for Anxiety* is concise, well organized, easy to read, and will likely be a lifeline of relief for many people. Chapman, Gratz, and Tull do a marvelous job of detailing the specific tools of DBT that can truly help readers to help themselves become more positive, able to cope, and successful in their relationships."

> —Denise D. Davis, PhD, clinical psychologist and founding fellow of the Academy of Cognitive Therapy

"This easy-to-read book provides practical and effective DBT strategies for anyone struggling with anxiety. The authors guide readers through a step-by-step process of dealing with stress and anxiety by building DBT skills like mindfulness and distress tolerance. A great resource for anxiety sufferers!"

—Pamela S. Wiegartz, PhD, author of *The Pregnancy and Postpartum Anxiety Workbook* and *The Worrier's Guide to Overcoming Procrastination*

"Chapman, Gratz, and Tull have written a wonderfully helpful guide to using the proven methods of DBT to overcome anxiety problems. In this excellent workbook, the authors clearly describe the key tools of DBT, then show you step by step how to apply these methods to problems such as worry, panic attacks, and social anxiety. I highly recommended this workbook for anyone seeking to conquer anxiety once and for all."

—Kevin L. Gyoerkoe, PsyD, director of The Anxiety and OCD Treatment Center in Charlotte, NC, and author of *10 Simple Solutions to Worry* and other books

The Dialectical Behavior Therapy Skills Workbook

— *for* —

Anxiety

Breaking Free from Worry, Panic,
PTSD & Other Anxiety Symptoms

ALEXANDER L. CHAPMAN, PhD
KIM L. GRATZ, PhD • MATTHEW T. TULL, PhD

New Harbinger Publications, Inc.

Distributed in Canada by Raincoast Books

Copyright © 2011 by Alexander L. Chapman, Kim L. Gratz, and Matthew T. Tull
New Harbinger Publications, Inc.
5674 Shattuck Avenue
Oakland, CA 94609
www.newharbinger.com

Acquired by Catharine Meyers; Cover design by Amy Shoup; Edited by Nelda Street

Library of Congress Cataloging-in-Publication Data

Chapman, Alexander L. (Alexander Lawrence)
  The dialectical behavior therapy skills workbook for anxiety : breaking free from worry, panic, PTSD, and other anxiety symptoms / Alexander L. Chapman, Kim L. Gratz, and Matthew T. Tull ; foreword by Terence M. Keane.
      p. cm.
  Includes bibliographical references.
  ISBN 978-1-57224-954-7 (pbk.) -- ISBN 978-1-57224-955-4 (pdf e-book)
  1. Anxiety disorders--Treatment--Popular works. 2. Dialectical behavior therapy--Popular works. I. Gratz, Kim L. II. Tull, Matthew T. III. Title.
  RC531.C46 2011
  616.85'220651--dc23
                              2011027693

14 13 12   10 9 8 7 6 5 4 3 2

To all the clients to whom I have taught DBT skills. You have taught and inspired me in many ways. Also, to A. J., a major source of inspiration for this book.

—A. L. C.

To the clients in my DBT skills groups, past and present. You bring these skills to life and inspire me to continue to engage with this material in new ways.

—K. L. G.

To all of my clients who struggle with anxiety and its disorders. I wish you peace and compassion for your journey through the uncertainty of life.

—M. T. T.

Contents

•   What Is Anxiety?   •   Anxiety vs. Anxiety Disorders   •   The Anxiety Disorders   •   Anxiety
and Avoidance   •   Conditions That Commonly Accompany Anxiety Disorders   •   Moving Forward

•   The Nuts and Bolts of CBT for Anxiety Disorders   •   Why DBT?   •   A Brief History of DBT
•   What Happens in DBT? DBT in a Nutshell   •   Moving Forward

Acknowledgments

I am grateful to so many people who have helped me to step onto and stay on this path I've taken, without whom this type of book would not be possible. I would like to thank all of my clients, who have taught me so much about how these skills work (and sometimes how they don't) to enhance their daily lives and bring them freedom and fulfillment. I got into DBT work back in graduate school, when I saw in one of my very first clients how powerful these skills can be and how much change is possible even in the midst of misery and despair. Since then, I have been compelled (somewhat obsessively and compulsively) to devote my career and much of my life to this work. One of my very favorite activities each week is the teaching of my DBT skills groups, and the best reward for this work occurs when I hear that people are using these skills to make meaningful changes in their lives. Each person I've worked with has taught me so much, and I thank you all for helping me to be in the best position to help others.

I am also grateful to my coauthors for taking this journey with me. I feel very fortunate to have Kim as a friend, colleague, and coauthor. You are one of the most skilled and compassionate people I've ever met, and these writing projects with you are a delight. I'd also like to thank Matt, without whom this book simply wouldn't exist. His expertise in anxiety disorders and clear, compassionate writing have been invaluable. I also have greatly appreciated the feedback and support (even when I have asked for deadline extensions for this book, which I must admit that I did twice!) of the editorial staff at New Harbinger, especially Catharine Meyers, Jess Beebe, and Kayla Sussell.

My parents, family, and mentors also have contributed so much to my life and work. I would like to thank my friend and colleague, Dr. Richard Farmer, for his guidance while I was a graduate student learning about treatments for anxiety and other disorders. I may not have appreciated those biweekly essays in your class at the time, but I sure do now. Dr. Marsha Linehan's wisdom has been essential to this work (I often hear her voice in my head whenever I write about, teach, or practice DBT), and I greatly appreciate her ongoing friendship and support of my work. I also would like to thank Dr. Tony Cellucci for his support, friendship, and guidance over the years. My parents have stuck with me and showed an unusual degree of acceptance and tolerance over the years, even years ago, when I tried to convince them that there was no point in my going to university. My wife, Katherine, has been a saint for supporting me throughout graduate school and putting up with all of my work, and for her amazing job as the mother of our two wonderful sons, Max and Quinn.

—Alex L. Chapman

I am eternally grateful to my clients, mentors, and coauthors for everything they have done and continue to do for me. This book would not have been possible without them. First, I would like to gratefully acknowledge the DBT skills group clients whose courage and strength I have been fortunate enough to witness over the years. I am humbled that they have invited me into their lives and trusted me to assist them in their journey toward more skillful behavior. They bring these skills to life and inspire me to continue to share this knowledge with others.

I would also like to acknowledge the DBT mentors, colleagues, and students I have had the pleasure and honor to work with over the years, from my mentor, Elizabeth Murphy, who sparked my ongoing passion for DBT and taught me how to truly engage with the skills and teach them in a flexible way, to the current colleagues and students on my DBT consultation team: Amee Epler, Jason Lavender, Mike Anestis, Nicole Weiss, and Lauren Baillie, who show me new ways of teaching and relating to these skills every day. Thank you for making this work so rewarding and fun. Thanks also to the supportive and skillful editorial staff at New Harbinger, especially Catharine Meyers, Jess Beebe, and Kayla Sussell. Their guidance throughout this process is greatly appreciated.

I would also like to express my gratitude to my coauthors on this project. First, to my book-writing partner and dear friend Alex Chapman, I am deeply thankful for our friendship and value the opportunity to continue to collaborate with you in this way. With each book we write together, I appreciate the process more and more. Second, I am eternally grateful to Matt Tull, my husband, for agreeing to join us in this endeavor and for contributing his vast knowledge of anxiety and related disorders to this book. We could not have done this without him. More importantly, my contributions to this book would not have been possible without Matt's ongoing love, support, patience, and encouragement (not to mention his amazing culinary skills). I am blessed and forever grateful to be able to share all aspects of my life with him and could not be happier to have him as my husband, partner, and consummate collaborator. Finally, I will always be grateful to my parents, Linda and Dave, for their steadfast support and unconditional love throughout my life, and to Daisy for bringing joy, peace, and love into our lives.

—Kim L. Gratz

Several people deserve recognition for their encouragement and support of me, which made this book possible. I would first like to acknowledge my mentor Lizabeth Roemer. Liz first introduced me to the world of anxiety disorders and greatly shaped my thinking about anxiety. She also opened my eyes to acceptance- and mindfulness-based treatments for anxiety disorders, which has had a tremendous influence on my life, both as a clinician and as a human being. I am grateful for the impact she has had on my development as a researcher and clinician.

I would also like to acknowledge my fellow authors, Alex Chapman and Kim Gratz. The idea of cowriting this book was (quite fittingly) anxiety provoking; however, it was a true pleasure to work with Alex and Kim. They made writing this book an easy and enjoyable experience, and I know it would not have been possible without their knowledge, experience, and dedication. I look forward to our future collaborations. I also very much appreciate the assistance and support of Jess Beebe, Kayla Sussell, and Catharine Meyers at New Harbinger Publications. Their comments have improved this book, and their support and excitement for this book was motivating. I am also thankful to my clients for sharing their lives and struggles with me. Above all else, I hope that this book will help people find peace in a world that is filled with many sources of anxiety, fear, and worry, allowing them to live the lives they want to live.

I also would like to thank my parents and my brother, Chris. Their unending, unconditional love, enthusiasm, and support throughout my life have always made me believe that anything is possible. They have instilled in me the values that have helped me get to this point in my life. I owe them much. Finally, I would like to acknowledge my wife, Kim (who also happens to be a coauthor of this book). The amount of love, support, and inspiration she provides is second to none. I have enjoyed being able to share this journey with her. I only hope that I live up to what she deserves in a husband, colleague, and friend.

—Matthew T. Tull

Foreword

Anxiety disorders are common, serious, yet eminently treatable. Progress in the treatment of anxiety disorders over the past thirty years is nothing short of remarkable. Each of the conditions responds to cognitive behavioral interventions tailored specifically for the problems at hand. This is truly outstanding news for patients suffering from these debilitating disorders, for therapists looking for ways to help patients presenting with these problems, and for the public health of this country and the world more broadly. *The Dialectical Behavior Therapy Skills Workbook for Anxiety* represents a welcome addition to the armamentarium available for clinicians looking to provide optimal care for their patients.

Conceived as a workbook for patients undergoing an active learning approach to the treatment of their disorder, this book is in fact far more. It provides people a context for understanding their recovery from the disabling features of anxiety. Understanding the context is helpful in encouraging people to move forward in treatment. They are not alone. For instance, in treating people who develop post-traumatic stress disorder (Keane, Marshall, and Taft 2006), we've learned that simply providing information on the diagnosis that characterizes their suffering presents a huge relief to the individual. Knowing that others have responded to traumatic life events in similar ways appears to represent a major advance for them.

Over the past twenty years, we've learned that the dialectical approaches stemming from Buddhist philosophies, when integrated with scientifically validated treatments (Linehan 1993), yield an augmentation of treatment effects. This improvement was initially visible with patients who suffered from personality disorders, but now we can say convincingly that these integrated treatments are enhancing the care of people with many different disorders, but in particular those that carry a major anxiety component. This workbook will contribute to a higher standard of care for patients, whether they use it on their own, with a therapist, or in a clinic.

How does one recover from panic, fear, phobias, PTSD, and a propensity to worry so much that it impedes one's ability to enjoy life? The process involves developing a sense of where you are in the recovery process, recognizing that there's more you want from your life, and refusing to be deterred from pursuing recovery. Psychologists call this *self-efficacy*: the capacity to see your way through the challenges before you.

Perhaps the most important concept in this workbook is mindfulness. A simple strategy conceptually, its effective use in your life becomes the architecture of recovery. Related to meditation, it offers a way of staying in the present when past, ineffective coping strategies foster looking toward the future. Mindfulness provides a coping strategy that facilitates positive present-moment performance and promotes a feeling of confidence beyond that which is customary. The key to strengthening mindfulness is practice. Beginning with the most elementary skills, one is quickly able to progress to applying mindfulness-based skills to the most complex and challenging experiences and settings. The rewards for applying the skills successfully are improvements in one's perspective on what is possible in life. Once these skills are mastered, you'll learn that you can do the things you think you cannot do.

What does the future hold for people who can learn to use dialectical skills in conjunction with other cognitive behavioral skills? The future is indeed bright. While today you are using a workbook for guiding your care, soon there will be internet-based facilitation of your treatment. The presence of the World Wide Web will permit the delivery of treatment on the spot and precisely when you need it. Smartphone-based applications are already available for some psychological conditions. More are under development. The present workbook, in its next iteration, will likely be available on the omnipresent smartphone so that reminders, lessons, and skills will be instantly available when you want them and when you might need them. This is the future of behavioral health care: therapy sessions that will work directly with you in your own home, work, and social environments. Social support will be delivered in person and electronically as one progresses systematically in overcoming obstacles to the enjoyment of life, pursuing goals, and gaining a firm sense of accomplishment.

As you explore *The Dialectical Behavior Therapy Skills Workbook for Anxiety*, you'll recognize that the book progresses in steps that are manageable for all those who are concerned that they can never overcome their anxiety. Drs. Chapman, Gratz, and Tull are clearly accomplished clinicians who are sensitive to the needs of their patients and are talented in organizing treatment hierarchically so that the skills appear in a sensible order, build on one another, and result in the availability of a balanced portfolio of skills to be used across situations, circumstances, and environments. Their work represents state-of-the-art care across the anxiety disorders and those conditions that occur concomitantly. Patients, clinicians, and health care more broadly will benefit from the careful attention to detail they've brought forward in this workbook.

—Terence M. Keane, PhD
director, Behavioral Science Division, National Center for Posttraumatic Stress Disorder
professor of psychiatry and psychology, Boston University

CHAPTER 1

Anxiety and Anxiety Disorders

Since you are reading this book, it is likely that you or someone you know struggles with anxiety. And, if this is the case, it is important for you to know that you are not alone. Anxiety problems are such a common experience for people that research on anxiety disorders has grown exponentially in the past three decades. Yet, despite how much we have learned about anxiety disorders, what causes them, and how to successfully treat them, people continue to struggle with the experience of anxiety. For example, a survey of almost ten thousand people across the United States found that with the exception of substance-use disorders, anxiety disorders are the most common mental health diagnosis. In fact, almost one-third of people surveyed had experienced at least one anxiety disorder at some point in their lives (Kessler et al. 2005).

So, why are anxiety disorders so common in our society? Well, it is difficult to identify one specific factor that explains why so many people struggle with anxiety disorders. It is likely that a number of different factors work together to explain why anxiety disorders are so common. Genetics (or inherited traits), experience and learning, stressful or traumatic events, and the basic uncertainty of life are all thought to play a role in the development of anxiety disorders (Barlow 2002b). However, another reason why anxiety disorders are so common may have to do with the fact that anxiety is such a common experience in everyday life.

Did you know that many of the anxiety disorders are actually more severe variants of common experiences? It's true. Take panic disorder, for example. *Panic disorder* is an anxiety disorder in which a person experiences frequent, out-of-the blue *panic attacks* (or episodes of intense fear and terror). Many people with panic disorder believe during a panic attack that they are dying or may be at risk of dying, and as a result, they may try to avoid the situations or activities that could trigger a panic attack, such as exercise. The large survey previously mentioned found that approximately 5 percent of people in the United States have had panic disorder at some point in their lifetimes (Kessler et al. 2005). However, what this survey doesn't tell us is that the experience of panic attacks is a very common one. Around 11 percent of people have experienced a panic attack in the past year, and 28 percent of people say that they have had a panic attack at some point in their lives (Kessler et al. 2006).

And this isn't just the case for panic attacks. Many other symptoms of common anxiety disorders are also common experiences among the general population. For example, worry (or thoughts about future stressful or anxiety-provoking situations), which is one of the main symptoms of generalized anxiety disorder, and checking and ordering behavior, a symptom of obsessive-compulsive disorder, are also quite common experiences (Tallis, Eysenck, and Mathews 1992; Radomsky and Rachman 2004).

Now, before you can understand what an anxiety disorder is, you need to first understand what anxiety is. In this chapter, we are going to take you through the basics of anxiety, including the symptoms of anxiety and how the normal, everyday experience of anxiety can turn into an anxiety disorder. We'll also describe some common unhealthy behaviors and mental health disorders that often go along with anxiety disorders. The goal of this chapter is to help you develop an understanding and awareness of your anxiety so we can better target it with the skills that we present later in this book. Let's get started.

WHAT IS ANXIETY?

When people talk about anxiety, they often lump together the experiences of anxiety and fear. Now, in some ways, this makes sense because these two emotions feel similar in the body and have similar functions. Both anxiety and fear are part of the human body's natural, hardwired alarm system, or the fight-or-flight response. However, they are actually different emotions. Before we go into the fight-or-flight response in more detail, let's examine how anxiety and fear differ.

Fear vs. Anxiety

Fear is more of a present-moment emotional experience. Fear is what you experience when you are actually in a stressful or threatening situation. For example, if you see a big, scary dog running at you, you will experience fear. Anxiety, on the other hand, is more of a future-focused emotion. If you are walking through a neighborhood where you were once chased by a big, scary dog, you probably will experience anxiety, because you may be worried about that nasty dog showing up again. Your body is putting you on alert for some possible future dangerous situation. Some researchers have even argued that anxiety may be better termed "anxious apprehension" (Barlow 2002a).

Another way to think about the difference between fear and anxiety is to think of what it's like to ride a roller coaster. Anxiety is what you experience as you get strapped into your seat and make your way toward that first gigantic hill. As you climb up that hill (and get closer and closer to your ultimate fall), your anxiety may increase, peaking as you reach the top of the hill and experience that slight pause right before you drop. Fear is what you experience as you rush down that hill. One emotion is about the anticipation of an event, and the other is about the actual experience of that event.

Now, both fear and anxiety serve a very important purpose: they tell you that you may be in a situation where there is risk of harm. That's good information to have! Anxiety also has an additional function, however. Specifically, anxiety can tell you that something matters to you, or is important and meaningful to you. Think about it. When you are about to interview for a job that you really want, you are probably more anxious than if you are about to interview for a job that you couldn't care less about. This is because the job matters to you. As another example, many people become anxious when they propose marriage to a romantic interest. This isn't because the situation is dangerous (at least, we hope not!). It is just because the situation has a tremendous amount of meaning. It matters.

The Fight-or-Flight Response

Now that we have described the difference between anxiety and fear, let's revisit the purpose of the fight-or-flight response. The fight-or-flight response has been around as long as human beings have been around. And, as we said before, it's the body's hardwired alarm system. If you think of the human body as a computer, the fight-or-flight response is an essential part of the operating system. You couldn't really function (or live that long) without it.

When you encounter a dangerous or threatening situation, this alarm system goes off, and your body goes through a number of changes. For example, during the fight-or-flight response, you may experience the following symptoms:

- An increase in heart rate

- Perspiration or sweating

- Narrowing of field of vision (also called "tunnel vision")

- Muscle tension

- Sensitive hearing

- Racing thoughts

- Shortness of breath

- Goose bumps

- Dry mouth

These experiences aren't random; they all serve a very important purpose. They prepare you for immediate action. They are preparing you either to flee the situation to avoid any harm or to fight if escape is not possible. In situations where fleeing or fighting is not necessarily a good option, your body may also freeze (kind of like a deer caught in a car's headlights).

This response is automatic. It occurs without thinking. This is important because it allows you to respond quickly when you are in a dangerous situation. For example, let's say that you are walking through the woods and come across a bear. Your fight-or-flight response will be activated, and you will likely freeze or flee. The sudden and automatic changes that your body goes through will help keep you alive in this dangerous situation. Now, if you had to think about the situation before the fight-or-flight response was activated, you would waste precious time. You would have to evaluate the size of the bear and the sharpness of its claws and teeth. And, by the time you figured all of that out, you would probably be supper for the bear! Therefore, the fight-or-flight response is incredibly helpful and adaptive. We likely wouldn't be alive as a species today without it.

Now, that's not to say that this system doesn't have its problems. That's because the fight-or-flight response hasn't really caught up to our species' ability to think, imagine, worry, perseverate, ruminate (or mull over past regrettable decisions), and so forth—all the wonderful mental activities that go along with being human. As a result, anxiety and fear may be activated when we evaluate or perceive a situation as threatening (regardless of whether it is actually dangerous). For example, if you are about to give a presentation to a large crowd and you evaluate yourself as ineffective or unprepared, or you think that the crowd may be hostile and unforgiving, you are more likely to experience anxiety, because you think the situation is threatening. It doesn't really matter whether or not your evaluations are accurate; your body responds the same: with fear, anxiety, and eventually avoidance.

How Do You Experience Fear and Anxiety?

Now that we have talked about the functions of anxiety and fear, let's start working toward increasing your awareness of these emotions. Being soundly aware of anxiety and fear will be important for learning the skills we'll teach you later in this book. You need to know what anxiety and fear feel like in order to identify them when they occur and then figure out the best skills to use in that situation.

To increase awareness of fear and anxiety, you need to break these feelings down into all of their parts. Emotions are actually made up of many different internal experiences, such as thoughts, bodily sensations, and behaviors. You can increase your awareness of fear and anxiety when they occur by identifying all the different pieces that make up the overarching experience labeled "anxiety" or "fear." In addition, you can also increase your awareness of when anxiety and fear are likely to occur by identifying the types of situations that bring up anxiety and fear. Exercise 1.1 will help you do all of this.

Exercise 1.1 Identify How You Experience Fear and Anxiety

Situations	Bodily Sensations	Thoughts	Action Tendencies	What You Actually Do

In the first column, labeled "Situations," we want you to identify any situation that brings up anxiety or fear for you. Now, keep in mind that anxiety-provoking situations can be in the outside world (for example, getting lost in a bad neighborhood or receiving an e-mail from your boss calling for a meeting with you right away) or inside your own body (for example, feeling short of breath or experiencing your heart racing). Remember, the fight-or-flight response really doesn't discriminate between inherently threatening situations and situations that we merely evaluate as threatening.

Next, in the column labeled "Bodily Sensations," we want you to write down any change that you notice in your body as a result of encountering an anxiety-provoking situation. For example, you may notice a racing heart, muscle tension, or shortness of breath. You may also notice some changes in how you perceive things in your environment. For example, when in a state of anxiety, sometimes people experience a narrowing of their vision or attention (tunnel vision) on the threatening object (such as a snake or spider) or sensation (such as an unpleasant thought or physical sensation). When in this state, people may have difficulty redirecting their attention away from the object (or person) perceived as threatening, or they may be more likely to notice other threatening aspects of their environments. Known as *attentional bias*, this is a very common experience in anxiety (MacLeod, Mathews, and Tata 1986). For instance, someone with social anxiety disorder who is giving a speech may be more likely to notice people in the audience who are yawning or frowning, even if there are many more people who look interested or are smiling.

In the next column, labeled "Thoughts," write down the type of thoughts that you experience when you are fearful or anxious. More often than not, your thoughts will revolve around the idea of threat or danger. Called *mood-congruent thinking*, this has to do with the fact that thoughts are strongly connected to emotions. Have you ever noticed that you have more positive thoughts when you are happy? How about more negative or unpleasant thoughts when you are sad or anxious? This is mood-congruent thinking. When in a state of anxiety or fear, we are much more likely to have thoughts that are in line with that emotional state. In addition, when anxious, we are also more likely to have memories of past anxiety-provoking events (Mitte 2008).

Now, if you are having a hard time identifying specific thoughts, ask yourself if you ever engage in "what if" thinking, or worry. Worry is a common experience in anxiety. *Worry* refers to future-oriented negative thoughts about a possible real-life problem or concern (Molina et al. 1998). Worry often stems from situations in which the outcome is uncertain or unpredictable (two aspects of a situation that will naturally bring up anxiety). For example, let's say that you lose your wallet. This would naturally be a stressful and anxiety-provoking event, and you may start to have thoughts such as *What if they use my credit card? What if they find out where I live and break into my house?* In many ways, worry can seem like an attempt to solve problems in order to create a sense of certainty and predictability. However, this process can backfire, especially when it is directed at future events, which are beyond our control. We'll discuss this in greater detail in chapter 6.

When you are anxious, you may also find yourself engaging in "all-or-nothing" thinking (also called "black-and-white" thinking). With all-or-nothing thinking, a person can get stuck in the idea that there are only two possible outcomes to a situation (Beck 1995). For example, if you are nervous about going out on a first date, you may think to yourself that if the date doesn't end up going perfectly, it will be a complete failure. Catastophizing is another way of thinking that often occurs with anxiety. As the name implies, you are *catastrophizing* when you expect the worst to happen or that certain experiences will have extreme negative consequences for your well-being (ibid.). For instance, some people with panic disorder believe that an increased heart rate is a sign that they are having a heart attack.

The next column is labeled "Action Tendencies." All emotions prepare you for some kind of action. As you discussed earlier, anxiety and fear prepare you to escape or avoid a distressing situation (or to fight or freeze if you can't escape the situation). This is what we want to capture within this column; when you experience anxiety and fear, what do you want to do? Do you have an urge to respond in a certain way? Do you want to run out of the room, scream, or disappear? In this column, write down what you feel like doing, as opposed to what you actually do.

Finally, in the last column, write down everything that you actually do when you feel afraid or anxious. How do you respond to the experience of anxiety and fear? Do you use deep breathing, meditation, prayer, or distraction (for example, reading a book like this one)? Do you drink or use drugs to try to escape these feelings? Do you eat comforting foods? Do you bite your nails or pick at the skin around them? Or, do you engage in more severe self-harm, such as cutting or burning yourself? In this column, make sure you write down everything you tend to do, both positive and negative, when you feel anxiety or fear. Identifying the positive coping strategies you are already using to manage anxiety is just as important as figuring out the things you do to manage anxiety that may not work as well. This exercise can help bring your attention to the strengths and skills you already have, in addition to those areas that you may need to work on.

When Do You Experience Anxiety?

Once you have completed exercise 1.1, you have accomplished the first step in treating your anxiety: understanding what anxiety and fear feel like for you. The next step is to increase your awareness of when anxiety tends to occur for you. You can do this through something called *self-monitoring*. As the name implies, we want you to monitor your experiences throughout each day. This exercise can provide you with some very important information.

Thoughts and feelings don't occur randomly (even though it may sometimes feel as if they do). Your internal experiences generally follow a set pattern, kind of like a habit. Therefore, by monitoring your internal experiences, you can start to understand the types of situations that generally bring on anxiety, as well as the times of day when you might be most vulnerable to experiencing anxiety. For example, if you find, through self-monitoring, that you tend to experience more intense anxiety in the morning, you can use this information to make sure you shore up your defenses during that time. You may schedule time in the mornings to practice certain skills that we'll discuss in this book, or you may schedule your morning to make sure that you don't have too much on your plate around that time.

Exercise 1.2 provides you with a basic self-monitoring form. It would be a good idea to make copies of this form so that you have a form for each day of the week. It is best to begin by monitoring your feelings and noting the times they came up for at least one week so that you can get as much information as possible. In the first column, write down the date; in the second, the time of day. Next, identify the situation you were in when the anxiety occurred. For example, were you at work, out with friends, driving your car, or at home alone? Next, rate the intensity of your anxiety on a scale from 0 to 100, with 0 being no or very low intensity and 100 being the most anxious you have ever been. Finally, rate your urge to avoid the anxiety or escape the situation you were in, using a scale from 0 (no urge to avoid) to 100 (strongest urge to avoid you have ever experienced), and indicate whether or not you did something to avoid or escape the anxiety.

Exercise 1.2 Anxiety Self-Monitoring Form

Date	Time	Situation	Intensity of anxiety (0–100)	Urge to avoid (0–100)	Did you avoid? (yes or no)

Keep this monitoring form with you throughout your day, and fill it out whenever you notice anxiety coming on. Filling it out as soon as you can after you have experienced anxiety will provide the best information, because the experience will be fresh in your mind. Of course, it is also important to keep in mind that monitoring your anxiety can itself be an anxiety-provoking experience. We're asking you to bring your attention to something that you might not always want to attend to, and the simple act of bringing attention to something unpleasant or uncomfortable can make it feel a little more intense. Now, this is very natural but, in the end, may actually help reduce your anxiety. However, we want you to be aware of this going into the exercise so that you won't be surprised if your anxiety feels a little more intense than usual. We also hope that this will not keep you from completing the exercise, as it is a really important step in learning to manage anxiety. Indeed, by increasing your awareness of the pattern of your anxiety, you may start to identify cues for your anxiety that you weren't aware of before. And the good news is that simply knowing more about the types of things that cue your anxiety or cause you to feel anxious can make your anxiety feel less unpredictable and, as a result, far less overwhelming.

ANXIETY VS. ANXIETY DISORDERS

Up until this point, we have been focusing on anxiety in general. And it is probably fairly clear by now that anxiety is not inherently problematic. It serves an important function and is necessary for day-to-day life. So, if we all have fear and anxiety (whether we want them or not), when do these emotions become a problem? In other words, when does the normal experience of anxiety and fear become a disorder? In a nutshell, anxiety becomes an anxiety disorder when the anxiety that you are experiencing is greater than what you might expect in a given situation, and when it begins to interfere with some aspect of your life.

For example, if your anxiety prevents you from forming desired relationships with people or meeting your responsibilities at work or school, this may be a sign that normal anxiety has shifted to a disorder of anxiety. In addition, if you find that you are engaging in unhealthy behaviors in an attempt to avoid or reduce your anxiety (such as drinking or using drugs), there is a good chance that you have a problem with anxiety. Here are some questions you may want to ask yourself to see if you may have a problem with anxiety.

Exercise 1.3 Do You Have a Problem with Anxiety?

	Yes	No
1. Do you avoid certain activities for fear that they may bring up symptoms of anxiety (for example, exercise, going to public places, watching certain television shows)?		
2. Do you tend to use alcohol or drugs to reduce your anxiety?		
3. Do you engage in any other unhealthy behavior to get relief from anxiety (for example, deliberate self-harm or binge eating)?		
4. Do you find that anxiety interferes with meeting your responsibilities at work?		
5. Do you have a hard time leaving your home because it is the only place where you really feel safe?		
6. Do you avoid watching certain television shows or movies because they bring up strong feelings of anxiety?		
7. Do you feel comfortable doing certain activities or going into certain situations only if you have taken steps to reduce your anxiety first (for example, taking medication or making sure you have a friend with you)?		
8. In some situations, do you experience anxiety that is stronger than what most people experience or what you'd normally expect in that situation?		
9. Do you worry so much that you have difficulty getting things accomplished or staying on task?		
10. Does your anxiety prevent you from getting sleep at night?		

Keep in mind that this is not an exhaustive list, and there are many ways anxiety can interfere with someone's life. In addition, simply checking "yes" on one of these items does not mean that you have an anxiety disorder. However, the list does provide some very common examples of ways in which anxiety can interfere with a person's life, and if you answered yes to any of these questions, it may be important to learn some skills for coping with anxiety so that it doesn't cause more problems in your life. And reading this workbook is an excellent place to start. Now let's turn our attention to the specific disorders of anxiety that people can have.

THE ANXIETY DISORDERS

There are six main anxiety disorders. Although we will describe most of these disorders in more detail later in this book, it is important to have a general idea of the many different ways in which simple anxiety can turn into an anxiety disorder.

Specific Phobia

The first anxiety disorder we will discuss is *specific phobia*. In this disorder, people experience such intense fear (even to the point of having a panic attack) when they come into contact with certain objects or situations that they take steps to avoid these objects or situations. Common specific phobias include *acrophobia* (fear of heights), *odontophobia* (fear of dentists), *arachnophobia* (fear of spiders), *ophidiophobia* (fear of snakes), and *claustrophobia* (fear of enclosed spaces).

Social Anxiety Disorder

Social anxiety disorder (also called "social phobia") is another anxiety disorder, in which a person experiences intense fear and anxiety in social situations due to a fear of negative evaluation (for example, being judged). And, just as with specific phobia, this intense fear often results in the avoidance of these social situations. The most common type of situation that people fear in social anxiety disorder is public speaking; however, there are other situations that people with social anxiety disorder may also fear, such as eating in front of people, urinating in public restrooms, or writing in front of people (Hofmann and Barlow 2002).

Panic Disorder

A person with *panic disorder* experiences frequent, out-of-the-blue panic attacks, as well as worry about the meaning or outcome of those panic attacks. For example, people with panic disorder might fear that a panic attack is a sign that they are dying or going crazy. As a result of these panic attacks, people with panic disorder often try to avoid activities or situations that might bring on symptoms of arousal, such as exercise or eating heavy meals. In extreme cases, people with panic disorder may fear leaving home, because it is the only place where they feel safe. If this happens, a person may be diagnosed with panic disorder with agoraphobia.

Obsessive-Compulsive Disorder

This disorder has received a fair amount of attention in the media recently. In *obsessive-compulsive disorder* (OCD), a person experiences intense, intrusive, and repetitive troublesome thoughts and ideas that might be viewed as strange and that are not about real-life problems. These out-of-the-ordinary thoughts and ideas are called *obsessions*. For example, people with this disorder may have persistent fears that they are going to accidentally poison their children, catch a disease, or harm someone else. As a result of these obsessions, people with OCD then engage in repetitive behaviors (or *compulsions*) to reduce the anxiety associated with those obsessions, such as excessive hand washing, ordering, checking, or performing mental rituals (such as counting).

Generalized Anxiety Disorder

Generalized anxiety disorder (GAD) is characterized by excessive, persistent, and uncontrollable worry about many different concerns. Sometimes people confuse GAD with OCD because both include the experience of repetitive thoughts. However, worry is different from obsession, because the worry in GAD is about real-life or daily concerns, such as finances, work, and relationships. Worry in GAD is actually viewed as an attempt to avoid or distract a person from more-upsetting and anxiety-provoking thoughts and feelings (Borkovec, Alcaine, and Behar 2004).

Post-Traumatic Stress Disorder

Finally, *post-traumatic stress disorder* (PTSD) is unique among the anxiety disorders, because it is the only one that requires people to have experienced some type of traumatic event before they can be diagnosed with it. PTSD is diagnosed when a person experiences a set of symptoms more than thirty days after exposure to a traumatic event. The symptoms of PTSD include intrusive thoughts and memories about the traumatic event (for example, flashbacks or feeling as if the event were happening all over again), avoidance of reminders of the traumatic event, difficulties experiencing positive emotions, feeling detached from others, and hyperarousal and hypervigilance (or always feeling on guard). If someone experiences these symptoms within one month after a traumatic event, we call the disorder *acute stress disorder*.

ANXIETY AND AVOIDANCE

Now, in addition to feelings of anxiety (which probably goes without saying), one behavior that is common among all of the anxiety disorders is the tendency or desire to avoid the feared object, experience, or situation. And, as much as the desire to avoid unwanted or unpleasant experiences makes sense and is a natural response, avoidance is actually the primary way in which anxiety disorders have a negative impact on a person's life. Specifically, anxiety and avoidance work together to form a vicious cycle that essentially traps a person. Let's discuss how this happens.

Earlier, we talked about how people who struggle with anxiety are more likely to notice or focus their attention on the very things they're afraid of in their internal (inside the body) or external (outside the body) environments. And if you think about it, this is actually something that can be protective. For example, if you are afraid of a dangerous object in your environment, it is probably in your best interest to make sure you keep an eye out for that object so that you can respond as quickly as possible when you see it. Unfortunately, however, this process also has its downside. That's because the more we pay attention to or increase our awareness of feared objects that we could encounter, the more likely we are to find them and be affected by them. For example, if you pay attention to your heartbeat, you are more likely to notice normal fluctuations in its rhythm. For someone with an anxiety disorder, such as panic disorder, this will bring up considerable anxiety.

Now, once you have your attention focused on a feared object or sensation, what happens next? Well, most people have trouble redirecting their attention away from the feared object or sensation. Therefore, most people will then take steps to try to get away from whatever is making them anxious. For example, if whatever you are afraid of is in your external environment, you could leave the situation. Or, if what you fear is an internal sensation, such as a thought or a bodily sensation, you could try to do something to get rid of your anxiety and bring down your arousal. This is how anxiety disorders can wreak havoc in your life. It is really common for people with anxiety disorders to get caught up in a vicious cycle in which they automatically (that is, without thinking) bring their attention to feared objects and sensations, have difficulty redirecting that attention away from them, and then try to avoid them.

Although trying to avoid things that make you anxious may seem to make a lot of sense (because who would want to feel anxious if he didn't have to?), one problem is that this is not actually possible. As you probably know, it is just not possible to avoid all anxiety-provoking situations, especially those that occur within your body. As a result, people with anxiety disorders often develop extreme avoidance behaviors in their efforts to feel safe or escape their anxiety, such as drinking heavily or never leaving home. Another problem that comes up when people get stuck in this cycle is that the more you avoid something, the more you learn that what you are avoiding should be feared (or why else would you avoid it?). Therefore, avoiding things we are afraid of can actually cause us to fear them even more.

Another problem is that avoidance really works only in the short term. In the long term, avoidance can actually make anxiety worse. This behavior perpetuates the cycle of anxiety and avoidance, making it stronger and stronger, until life becomes all about trying to get rid of anxiety.

CONDITIONS THAT COMMONLY ACCOMPANY ANXIETY DISORDERS

Not surprisingly, we often see a number of other mental health problems develop alongside anxiety disorders. Therefore, we will finish out this first chapter with a quick review of different disorders that often go along with anxiety disorders.

Substance-Use Disorders

People with anxiety disorders often struggle with some form of substance use, such as smoking (Morissette et al. 2007), drinking alcohol excessively (Sabourin and Stewart 2008), or using drugs (Tull et al. 2008). For example, people with social anxiety disorder have been found to be at high risk of alcohol abuse (Kessler et al. 1996), and people with PTSD often have problems with drug abuse (Tull et al. 2008).

So, why do people with anxiety disorders often struggle with substance use? Well, there are a number of theories, but the most popular theory is called the *self-medication hypothesis* (Robinson et al. 2009). This theory says that people who struggle with anxiety and have anxiety disorders may use controlled substances as a way to reduce their anxiety. Basically, according to this theory, using controlled substances is a way of avoiding or getting rid of anxiety. Of course, as people continue to rely on controlled substances to manage their anxiety, they can actually become more and more anxious, in addition to developing an addiction to the substances they are using. So, although this may work in the short term, it usually backfires in the long term, resulting in an addiction to the substance and all of the problems associated with that, in addition to even more anxiety than they were struggling with to begin with.

Depression

Depression and anxiety disorders go hand in hand. In fact, studies have found that well over half of the people who have had an anxiety disorder in their lifetimes have also had major depression (Brown and Barlow 2002). Depression is especially likely to go along with PTSD, GAD, and OCD (Brown et al. 2001). So, what might explain this? Well, for one, there is a great deal of overlap between anxiety disorders and major depression. For example, both depression and anxiety disorders share the experience of intense negative emotions (Brown and Barlow 2002). Second, a lot of the same risk factors that may lead to anxiety disorders have also been found to lead to depression, so people who experience these types of risk factors (for example, life stressors) may be more likely to develop both depression and anxiety disorders (Barlow, Chorpita, and Turovsky 1996). Finally, it is easy to see how the symptoms of anxiety disorders could lead to depression (Brown and Barlow 2002). For example, feeling confined to the house for fear of having a panic attack if you went outside would probably get in the way of your living a life that is meaningful to you.

Often, people with anxiety disorders spend so much time trying to avoid the things they are afraid of that they do not have the time or energy to do things that matter to them. And, as mentioned, sometimes the things that matter to people are the very things that bring up anxiety and fear; therefore, if they avoid the things they fear, people may end up having to avoid all of the things in their lives that matter to them. And it's pretty easy to see how this could lead to depression.

Eating Disorders

Eating disorders are also quite common among people with anxiety disorders. Studies have found that 12 percent of people with anxiety disorders have an eating disorder (Swinbourne and Touyz 2007), and there is evidence that the experience of an anxiety disorder leads to the development of an eating disorder (Brewerton et al. 1995; Godart et al. 2003). Eating disorders generally take the form of either *anorexia nervosa* (restricting food intake to such a degree that the person is severely underweight) or *bulimia nervosa* (a cycle of bingeing and purging in which large amounts of food are consumed and then eliminated, through some combination of vomiting, overexercising, or abusing laxatives). Just like with substance-use problems and depression, there is a very good reason why so many people with anxiety disorders might struggle with an eating disorder.

Basically, like substance use, the unhealthy eating behaviors seen in eating disorder diagnoses may be used to alleviate or reduce symptoms of anxiety. For example, studies have found that disordered eating behaviors, such as bingeing and purging, may be used to cope with emotional distress and relieve negative emotions (Whiteside et al. 2007). Think about it: eating is one of the most common ways people soothe themselves, and even people who do not have an anxiety disorder often use food to provide comfort during times of stress. Therefore, it makes sense that people who struggle with intense anxiety may be likely to turn to food for comfort.

In addition, given that many people with anxiety disorders feel as if their lives are out of their control and have difficulties coping with uncertainty and unpredictability, another reason an eating disorder like anorexia nervosa is common among people with anxiety disorders may be that this disorder can provide people with a sense of control. Now, unfortunately, this sense of control is an illusion, as eating disorders can actually take on a life of their own and get out of control. However, in the short term, purposely restricting food intake and choosing not to eat can provide people with a sense of control over at least some aspect of their lives. Thus, for people with anxiety disorders who feel as if their lives are out of control, food restriction may be one way to try to establish a sense of control (Shafran 2002).

Borderline Personality Disorder

Last, but not least, is *borderline personality disorder* (BPD). BPD is a disorder characterized by instability in emotions, thinking, relationships, identity, and behavior. People with BPD find it difficult to control impulsive or self-destructive behaviors, and often they have chaotic and upsetting interpersonal relationships. They also sometimes struggle with their identities, not knowing exactly who they are or what they're like. Finally, people with BPD struggle with their emotions and often experience their emotions as intense, uncontrollable, overwhelming, and threatening. One of the emotions that people with BPD struggle with the most is anxiety. In fact, more than 80 percent of people with BPD also have an anxiety disorder (Zanarini et al. 1998), with the most common ones being social anxiety disorder, panic disorder, and PTSD (Lieb et al. 2004). For example, studies have found that one-quarter to one-half of those with BPD also experience social anxiety disorder, one-third to one-half also experience panic disorder, and approximately one-half also experience PTSD (ibid.).

So, why do BPD and anxiety disorders go hand in hand? Well, one reason is that BPD and some of the anxiety disorders are actually caused by some of the same experiences. For example, childhood abuse is one of the primary causes of both PTSD and BPD. In addition, some of the same personality traits thought to cause anxiety disorders have also been found to increase the risk of BPD. For example, one personality trait that is strongly linked to anxiety disorders is *anxiety sensitivity*, or the tendency to fear anxiety symptoms due to beliefs that these symptoms will have negative consequences (Reiss 1991). Studies have shown that anxiety sensitivity increases the risk of developing an anxiety disorder. As with childhood abuse, however, there is also evidence that anxiety sensitivity may play a role in BPD (Gratz, Tull, and Gunderson 2008).

In addition, it is also the case that some of the symptoms of BPD may develop in response to strong feelings of anxiety. For example, one of the diagnostic criteria of BPD, deliberate self-harm (intentionally harming oneself physically), is often used to reduce feelings of anxiety and stress (Chapman, Gratz, and Brown 2006). Likewise, other impulsive and risky behaviors that are common among people with BPD may also be used to manage unpleasant emotions in some anxiety disorders, such as engaging in risky or impulsive behaviors (behaviors that are done without thinking of the consequences) (Tull et al. 2009).

MOVING FORWARD

Congratulations! You've made it through the first chapter of this workbook, and you are well on your way to understanding your anxiety and the ways in which you can begin to limit its negative impact on your life. Getting started can often be the hardest part of making any change in your life, and by connecting with and recognizing your difficulties with anxiety, you have overcome a major hurdle. Remember to take all the time you need to go through the exercises in this chapter. Increasing your awareness and understanding of your anxiety will provide you with a strong foundation on which to build all of the other skills we present in this workbook. From this point forward, we will start talking about the different ways in which anxiety can be treated, including the approach we take in this workbook.

CHAPTER 2

Overview of Cognitive Behavioral Therapy and Dialectical Behavior Therapy

In the last chapter, we provided you with a quick overview of anxiety, its purpose, and how people can develop anxiety disorders. Now that you know a little more about what you're dealing with, we will move on to talk about treatment. Here, we give you an overview of cognitive behavioral therapy (CBT) and dialectical behavior therapy (DBT) and discuss a couple of important things to keep in mind as you go through the rest of the book, along with some exercises that you might find useful. In this chapter, we'll cover the following:

- An overview of CBT for anxiety disorders

- An overview of DBT, its history, and why it can be helpful for anxiety problems

As we will discuss later in this chapter, the treatments with the best scientific evidence for anxiety problems tend to be cognitive behavioral therapies, or CBTs. CBTs help you recover from anxiety problems by changing anxiety-provoking thinking patterns and behaviors that maintain anxiety, and by teaching you new skills or strategies to cope with anxiety. These CBTs are extremely effective for many people with a variety of anxiety disorders, such as social anxiety disorder, post-traumatic stress disorder, obsessive-compulsive disorder, and panic disorder, with as many as 80 percent of people becoming symptom free after treatment, as reported in some studies (Craske and Barlow 2008).

THE NUTS AND BOLTS OF CBT FOR ANXIETY DISORDERS

CBT is based on the idea that a combination of thinking patterns, behaviors, and events in your environment can contribute to and maintain anxiety problems. CBT therapists address these problems in several ways, often including cognitive therapy, exposure therapy, and training in coping and anxiety management skills.

Cognitive Therapy

In cognitive therapy the therapist helps you to monitor, evaluate, and change thinking patterns that contribute to anxiety problems. Some of these thinking patterns involve overestimating the risk of danger in certain situations. For example, if you are afraid of public speaking, you might overestimate the risk that if you were to speak in front of people, you would be humiliated, judged, or criticized. If you are afraid of spiders, you might overestimate the risk that a spider might jump up and bite you if you got anywhere near it (one of the authors of this book shares similar concerns!). Certain that danger is lurking around the corner, you might become afraid and anxious in a variety of situations. Other thinking patterns addressed in CBT include thoughts that you are unable to cope with anxiety-provoking situations (that you are simply incapable or that it would be too much for you to cope with), catastrophizing thoughts (thinking that things will end up horribly, such as if you went to a party, people might ask you why you came and encourage you to leave), among others. Any of these types of thinking patterns, from a CBT perspective, can ramp up your anxiety. Therefore, in CBT, therapists often use cognitive therapy to help you learn how to change your thinking patterns and develop more useful or accurate thoughts.

Exposure Therapy

In exposure therapy, the therapist helps you to face situations, objects, or events that you are afraid of and would normally avoid. You might wonder, why on earth would you want to do that? Well, as we mentioned in chapter 1, one of the factors that keeps anxiety disorders going is avoidance of objects, situations, events, people, and even thoughts or emotions. If you are afraid of going to parties and avoid them entirely, you never have the chance to learn that parties are not as awful or threatening as you might think. Instead of letting you avoid parties and keep your fear alive, exposure therapy is based on the idea that you can teach yourself to be less afraid by purposely facing things of which you are afraid. In exposure therapy, you purposely enter situations of which you're afraid over and over again until your fear diminishes. If you are afraid of high places (acrophobia), your therapist might take you up to high places, have you notice and monitor how you feel, and keep you there until your anxiety diminishes. Then, you'd return to that place during the next session and keep doing this until you realize that you are a lot less afraid of being in high places. Now, one thing to keep in mind is that exposure therapy doesn't work if you have a really good reason to be afraid. If you are afraid of playing with black mamba snakes, then we suggest that you avoid playing with those snakes, because that's a perfectly healthy fear!

Coping Skills

CBT also often involves training in anxiety-management skills. The idea is that if you struggle with anxiety problems, it can be useful for you to have a few tools you can use to calm yourself down when your anxiety becomes overwhelming. Some of the most common skills include breathing retraining and progressive muscle relaxation. *Breathing retraining* involves changing how you breathe: instead of breathing shallowly, drawing your breath by arching your shoulders and moving your chest, in breathing retraining you draw air in deeper through your abdomen or diaphragm area. By doing this, you can reduce your heart rate and other symptoms of anxiety, and change the ratio of carbon dioxide to oxygen in your bloodstream. *Progressive muscle relaxation* is another common skill taught in CBT for anxiety disorders. This skill involves systematically tensing and relaxing your muscles and is designed to help you feel calmer and notice the difference between holding tension in your muscles and having loose, relaxed muscles. Both breathing retraining and progressive muscle relaxation are parts of most treatments for anxiety disorders and can be quite helpful.

Exercise 2.1 Try Diaphragmatic Breathing Right Now!

You can practice diaphragmatic breathing right now if you'd like: Put one hand on your chest and one hand on your abdomen. Now, slow down and deepen your breathing, and when you breathe, try your best to make your hand on your abdomen move up and down more than your hand on your chest. Just focus on your breathing and how it feels to draw in the air and exhale it. You can even say to yourself *inhale* with each inhalation, and *exhale* with each exhalation. Try this for ten minutes and see what it feels like. Do your best, while you're doing this, just to let anxious thoughts come and go, and simply focus on your breathing. Rate your anxiety on a scale from 0 to 10 (where 0 means no anxiety and 10 means extreme anxiety) before and after this exercise, and see if you notice any difference.

Anxiety before: _____   Anxiety after: _____

Even though our focus in this book is on DBT, we bring up CBT for a couple of very important reasons. Perhaps the most important reason is that you will be much better able to help yourself with your anxiety problems if you know about available treatments that work. If you had asthma and knew nothing at all about its treatments, you could go to a doctor who prescribes bananas and omega-3 fatty acids, and go merrily on your way, only to find yourself wheezing, gasping, and wondering why this "prescription" isn't helping you, as you scarf down a half-dozen bananas and a can of salmon in a desperate attempt to open your airways. Well, okay, we're exaggerating a bit! But we have seen many people who had no idea what types of treatments really work for anxiety disorders. As a result, they have sometimes spent time and money on treatments that simply did not work. Beyond knowing what treatments to seek, once you know a bit about effective treatments for anxiety disorders, you might have a clearer idea of what DBT adds to these treatments and how, even if you are already in a treatment that helps you, DBT may give you some added benefits.

WHY DBT?

Now, you might be wondering what DBT adds and why we need it, if these other treatments are available and work so well. Simply put, DBT is a type of CBT, but it offers strategies for dealing with anxiety that regular CBT treatments do not usually include. Some of these strategies are as follows:

- Mindfulness skills to learn how to live in the present moment, paying attention to your thoughts, emotions, and experiences in the here and now

- Acceptance skills to learn how to accept yourself, other people, and emotions you have a hard time tolerating or managing

- Interpersonal skills (basically, assertiveness) to learn how to talk to people, assertively get your needs met, and determine when and how to ask for what you want and to say no to unwanted requests

- Emotion regulation skills to help you identify all of your emotions, not just anxiety, and learn how to manage them

DBT (Linehan 1993a; 1993b) was originally developed by Dr. Marsha Linehan at the University of Washington to help suicidal women. However, Dr. Linehan soon found out that many of the suicidal women she was treating had many other problems as well. In particular, many of these women met criteria for BPD (if you want to learn more about BPD or if you think that you or a loved one might have this disorder, you might be interested in Alex and Kim's book *The Borderline Personality Disorder Survival Guide: Everything You Need to Know about Living with BPD* (New Harbinger Publications, 2007). And over time, DBT has come to be the most scientifically supported therapy for people who struggle with BPD.

Now, as you might remember from chapter 1, BPD and anxiety disorders often go hand in hand. Therefore, a lot of people with anxiety disorders have been treated with DBT; they just happened to have BPD as well. However, beyond the fact that many people with BPD have anxiety disorders, evidence suggests that many DBT strategies and skills may be very helpful for a lot of the problems that go along with anxiety disorders. For example, studies (see Robins and Chapman 2004, for a review) have found that DBT can be quite useful for:

- Anxiety disorders and symptoms

- Depression

- Substance-use problems

- Eating disorders

- Trauma

In fact, the skills taught in DBT are so practical and based in such common sense that almost anyone could potentially benefit by at least knowing something about them.

A BRIEF HISTORY OF DBT

At the time that Dr. Linehan began to develop DBT, most people were using cognitive or behavioral techniques to help suicidal women. The idea was that if they could change the hopeless thoughts they were having about their lives or change their actions (for instance, by increasing enjoyable activities or getting more social support), their lives would improve and they would no longer be suicidal. Dr. Linehan found out, however, that many of the patients she worked with did not like the fact that treatment focused so much on what they had to change (such as their thoughts and behaviors).

These patients felt that the message they were receiving was that their problems were their own fault. It's as if you were stranded in a dark, frightening forest with animals stalking you night and day, and a forest guide came along to tell you that you wouldn't be there in the first place if you had really thought things through. Or maybe you wouldn't be so upset about it if you decided to think about it differently (for example, *What an exciting game of chase!*). Therefore, Dr. Linehan soon realized that she had to find new ways to show her clients that she accepted them for who they were, and also to help them accept themselves, before they could make meaningful changes. You have to stop beating yourself up and accept that you took a wrong turn and ended up in the forest before you can really work to find your way out.

WHAT HAPPENS IN DBT? DBT IN A NUTSHELL

Ordinarily DBT is a fairly involved treatment with several different parts to it, including individual therapy, telephone consultation, a therapist consultation team, and group skills training. Although we will focus on the skills in this book, it can be helpful to know about the other aspects of DBT:

- **Individual therapy:** Individual therapy in DBT takes the form of a one-hour session each week, during which the therapist uses CBT to help you reach goals that are important to you, reduce behaviors you want to reduce, manage problems such as depression and anxiety (among others, if relevant, such as substance use, eating disorders, or self-harm behaviors), and, often, improve relationships.

- **Telephone consultation:** Telephone consultation in DBT involves the individual therapist's being available to you in between sessions for as-needed phone calls (or for conversations by e-mail or text messages) to help you deal with crises or emergencies, learn to apply new skills in your everyday life, and manage issues that have come up in your relationship with your therapist.

- **Therapist consultation team:** The therapist consultation team involves a weekly meeting, much like a support and supervision group, of DBT therapists that focuses on how the therapists can be as effective as possible with their clients, manage the stress that goes along with being a therapist, and learn how to get better at what they do.

- **DBT skills training:** Clients learn practical skills in the areas of mindfulness, interpersonal effectiveness, emotion regulation, and distress tolerance in a weekly group session, usually involving two therapists and six to ten clients.

This last component of DBT, the DBT skills, is what we will focus on in this book. Throughout most of this book, we will focus on how you can use DBT skills to effectively deal with anxiety and anxiety problems and improve your life in other ways, such as by increasing your sense of joy and happiness, improving your relationships, and achieving goals that are important to you. The four different sets of skills that are taught in DBT are (Linehan 1993b):

- **Mindfulness skills:** These skills help you learn to pay attention to your experiences in the here and now and to live more in the present moment.

- **Emotion regulation skills:** These skills help you learn to identify and better understand your emotions; reduce your vulnerability to negative emotions (such as anxiety); and learn strategies to manage, accept, or change your emotions.

- **Interpersonal effectiveness skills:** These skills help you learn to identify your goals in interpersonal situations and then, from there, figure out how to get your needs met, ask for what you want, and refuse unwanted requests while enhancing your relationships with others.

- **Distress tolerance skills:** These skills help you learn to tolerate and deal with overwhelming emotions, thoughts, or situations that are hard to change, by learning to think through your options in a crisis; use distraction or self-soothing; and accept yourself, your situation, and your experiences for what they are.

In chapter 3, we will give you a road map to these skills, what they are, and how they can help. Then, in future chapters, we will help you figure out how to use the skills to manage anxiety-related problems, such as:

- Obsessions and compulsive behavior

- Anxiety, stress, and tension

- GAD, worry, and rumination

- PTSD

- Social and other phobias

- Panic disorder and agoraphobia

Before we move on to chapter 3 and cover the skills in more detail, we want to give you a few important things to keep in mind as you learn how to use DBT for anxiety problems. Knowing these points will help you to have the right, or most effective, mind-set as you learn the skills.

Balance Your Efforts to Accept and Change Your Problems

In DBT, balance is incredibly important. In fact, balance is central to the theory that drives this treatment: dialectical theory. *Dialectics* basically means tension between opposing forces, sort of like good versus bad, negative versus positive charges, thesis versus antithesis, right versus wrong, cold versus hot.

In DBT, the opposing forces are acceptance and change (Linehan 1993a). Acceptance means to allow your emotions, thoughts, and circumstances to simply be what they are, just for now, without struggling to change, modify, escape, or get rid of them. To change, in contrast, means to alter your emotions, thoughts, and circumstances.

DBT is dialectical, because in DBT we are always trying to strike an effective balance between acceptance and change (ibid.). We believe that, in order to deal effectively with emotional difficulties, you need to balance acceptance and change. If you focus too much on changing your emotions, thoughts, and situations, you can experience problems.

Dialectics, then, has to do with the idea that in any situation, you could choose to accept what's happening, to change what's happening, or some combination of both. The challenge is in figuring out what you need to accept and what would be best to change. This is a lot like the Serenity Prayer (by Reinhold Niebuhr) used in Alcoholics Anonymous: you need the wisdom to know the difference between what you can change and what you can't, when to accept, and when to change.

In DBT, maybe even more so than in other treatments, we spend a lot of time helping people find ways to balance acceptance and change and find some kind of synthesis or combination of the two that works best.

Let's say that you are depressed. You have been spending a lot of time in bed, avoid phone calls, feel empty and sad much of the time, have difficulty concentrating, and have a lot of negative thoughts about yourself. A synthesis or combination of acceptance and change might include:

- Accepting that you are depressed, that you feel sad and empty much of the time, and that you have been and are currently inactive.

- Deciding to slowly get up and drag yourself (with help, hopefully) out of depression by getting active, solving some of the problems that keep you depressed, and making important changes in your life.

Here are a few other examples of this combination, synthesis, or balance of acceptance and change:

- When a relationship has suffered, you often have to acknowledge and accept the fact (accept) that you have hurt someone and feel guilty before you can effectively repair the relationship (change).

- To deal with OCD, you have to both accept that you have obsessive thoughts and work to change your repetitive compulsive behaviors (checking, engaging in rituals, hand washing, and so forth).

- The best way to change panic symptoms is often to accept, sit with, and experience (accept) your panic symptoms, rather than try actively to escape or change them.

- Sometimes the best way to accept and deal with the overwhelming stress of having too many things to do is to change things by breaking your tasks into smaller, more manageable steps (change the tasks).

- If you're afraid of public speaking, sometimes the best way to get through it is to accept the anxiety and fear you experience, then change the focus of your attention so that you're paying more attention to your audience than to your own bodily symptoms (possibly the last thing you'd want to do!).

- Sometimes the best way to deal with worry (for example, about financial, relationship, or health problems) is to accept that you're worrying that something bad might happen, improve your skills at estimating whether something bad will happen, and change or prevent what you can.

- If you deal with obsessive religious thoughts, such as that you might offend God if you wore a particular type of shirt, sometimes the best way to break free of such thoughts is to acknowledge that you really don't know what might happen, and then wear the shirt anyway, on purpose.

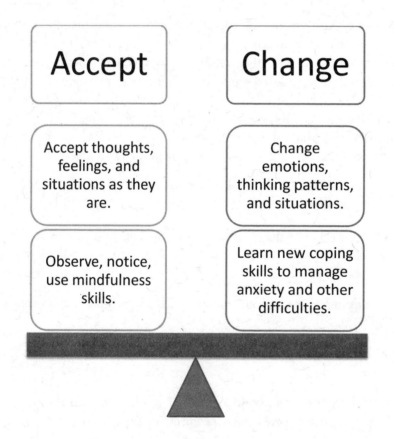

Figure 2.1   **How to Balance Your Efforts to Accept and Change Your Problems**

Do Your Best to Avoid Avoiding

Another suggestion we have is for you to start working on reducing your avoidance of unwanted emotions, thoughts, and situations. As we discussed in chapter 1, too much avoidance can be a big problem when it comes to anxiety problems. In DBT and through the DBT skills you'll learn in this book, you will learn several strategies to help you stop avoiding your emotions and thoughts. Indeed, David Barlow, a leading expert in the treatment of anxiety disorders, has said that one of the most important things people with anxiety problems can do is to learn to stop avoiding their emotions (Barlow, Allen, and Choate 2004). Now, you might be thinking, *Yeah, right! You try to live with this tension and anxiety every day, and then tell me how much you'd like to stop avoiding it!*

That would be perfectly understandable. As discussed in chapter 1, when you experience really uncomfortable feelings on a regular basis, it is natural to want to avoid them and try to do so. All things considered, and with some exceptions, most of us just don't like to feel discomfort. And, anxiety and fear are uncomfortable.

For instance, if you are anxious in social situations or when speaking in public, you might avoid anxiety by staying away from people and avoiding all opportunities to talk in front of people. These strategies work in the short term, in that you probably feel calmer and less anxious when you are at home in your living room than when you're around people. That's why people keep avoiding situations that trigger anxiety; it feels better in the short term to do so. This is called *negative reinforcement*: you keep doing a behavior (staying at home), because it takes away something you don't want (anxiety).

The problem is that avoidance just keeps the fear and anxiety alive. If you never go to a party, see friends, or talk in front of people, you never get the chance to learn that whatever you were afraid of (such as humiliation or embarrassment) usually doesn't happen or isn't all that bad when it does happen. So, the fear and anxiety are kept alive. If, instead, you stopped avoiding anxiety-provoking situations, your brain would learn, over time, to stop pressing the panic-anxiety-fear button, provided that nothing really bad happened.

Another problem with avoidance is that there is often a *rebound effect*. This effect is seen when the very thoughts you try hardest to avoid are the same ones that seem to keep coming back. Well, in some research studies, people have found that when you try to suppress or avoid your thoughts, they tend to come back with a vengeance (Wegner, Erber, and Zanakos 1993). It's not fair, we know, but it's true.

Suppressing or avoiding thoughts and emotions is a lot like trying to prevent a flood of people from pushing through your front door into your living room. As long as you keep watch and push against the door, you might be able to hold them off for a while. But, if a boiling kettle in the kitchen distracts you, or if you try to brush your teeth at the same time, those people might just make it through that door. In a similar way, if you get interrupted and stop trying to avoid your thoughts or emotions, they can come flooding through.

The other option, then, would be to bolt the door shut, build a big brick wall, and board up all the windows and entryways in your house. The problem with that option, however, is that you may never get out of your own house. And, when it comes to thoughts and feelings, it's impossible to completely block them out without blocking out most of your life.

In contrast, if you were to just let the people in through the door one by one and really look at who is coming in, you might learn to deal with them or at least to face them without quite as much fear. This would be an example of acceptance.

MOVING FORWARD

To summarize, DBT is a cognitive behavioral therapy that also includes several helpful skills beyond regular CBT. When learning DBT skills, it is important to work on balancing how much you accept your problems versus change your problems, particularly when it comes to anxiety problems. In addition, it is also important to try your best to reduce your avoidance of emotions and thoughts, and try to use other ways to cope, ways that don't involve avoiding. In the next chapter, we discuss skills that will help you do just that: accept and tolerate your emotions and thoughts, and stop avoiding them.

CHAPTER 3

DBT Mindfulness and Distress Tolerance Skills

Now that you have an idea of the types of anxiety symptoms and related problems we will help you with in this workbook, as well as a general idea of what DBT is all about, it is important to have a good understanding of the DBT skills that we will use to address your anxiety symptoms. Therefore, in this and the next chapter, we will begin to provide you with a road map to the DBT skills.

Remember how we talked about avoidance being one of the things that fuels anxiety problems and disorders? Well, in this chapter, we will introduce you to two sets of DBT skills that can help you to break harmful avoidance patterns and learn to accept, tolerate, and be present each moment in your life, even when things are tremendously difficult: mindfulness and distress tolerance skills. In this chapter, we will provide a description of what these skills are all about and how they might help you, as well as a couple of practice exercises to get you started with them.

The purpose of this chapter and the next is to provide you with a basic understanding of what DBT skills entail and how they generally work. How each skill can be applied to specific anxiety symptoms will be discussed in later chapters.

DBT MINDFULNESS SKILLS

Through DBT mindfulness skills, you learn to pay attention to your emotions, thoughts, and experiences in the present moment. Used in several different types of treatments and with roots in both Eastern and Western spiritual practices, mindfulness is simply paying attention to your experiences in the here and now (Kabat-Zinn 1990; Linehan 1993b). You don't have to meditate or sit for long hours on an uncomfortable mat with incense burning in the corner to be mindful, nor do you have to become a Zen master; you just have to be willing to awaken your mind to what is happening right here, right now.

Mindfulness Is the Foundation for the Other Skills

One of the reasons we bring up mindfulness first is that you need it to effectively use any of the other skills we cover in this book. Mindfulness is a fundamental skill that helps you put the other skills into action, because mindfulness is all about paying attention to what you are doing and experiencing. When you are first learning new skills, you have to be mindful, pay close attention to what you're doing, and maybe even describe to yourself the steps you're taking in applying the skills. In this way, mindfulness is like the foundation of a house; you build the rest of the DBT skills and strategies on top of it.

Perhaps because mindfulness is so important in DBT, many of our clients have said that it was the most helpful skill they ever learned. In fact, people have told us that simply practicing these skills and learning to be more present in their daily lives can be life changing. Moreover, when it comes to anxiety, as you will see in later chapters, there are many benefits to your learning mindfulness skills.

Being Mindful in Daily Life

Sometimes, the best way to practice mindfulness is to simply choose an everyday activity and do it mindfully, paying attention to what is happening right now, rather than getting caught up in thoughts, concerns, or worries about the past or future. For example, there are different ways you can walk down the street on a beautiful autumn day:

- **Stuck in your head:** One way to walk down the street would be for your body to do the walking and moving, while you think about other things. Perhaps you're working out your finances, worrying about a test or things that might go wrong in the future, or thinking a lot about things that went wrong in the past. Perhaps you're consumed with anxious or distressing thoughts that pull you away from the present and make it hard to even notice your surroundings. That's one way to walk down the street.

- **Just getting where you're going:** Another way to walk down the street would be to focus on getting where you are going. This would involve walking quickly, trying to beat lights at crosswalks, dodging people as they get in your way, avoiding eye contact and random conversations with people, looking straight ahead, and focusing on where you are going and how to get there. This is what mindfulness expert Dr. Jon Kabat-Zinn would call being in "doing" mode, in which you're totally focused on getting something accomplished rather than experiencing your life in the present moment.

- **Mindfully:** Another way to walk down the street would be to awaken your mind to your surroundings: watching the leaves as they fall gently to the sidewalk; noticing the colors in the trees, the shapes and styles of the buildings you pass, and the way the light reflects off the plants, trees, and passing cars; feeling the breeze on your face; and noticing how your legs feel when walking, what the pavement or trail feels like under your feet, and so on. This would be more like what Dr. Kabat-Zinn calls being in "being" mode, in which you're fully in the present moment, paying attention to and experiencing what is happening in the here and now.

Oddly enough, the third way of walking, using mindfulness skills, sounds simple but is probably the hardest of the three. It can be a lot easier and feel more natural to be in your head the whole time, not even paying attention to what's right in front of you. In fact, this is how many people spend much of their lives—in their heads. But this third way of walking is how you would walk if you were practicing mindfulness, and it would help you better connect with positive and rich present-moment experiences, something people often miss out on by being in their heads.

The Basics of DBT Mindfulness Skills

In DBT, there are several different types of mindfulness skills, but the basic idea in mindfulness is to bring your mind to the present and pay attention to your experiences in the here and now. Often the first step in mindfulness is to simply *pay attention to* and *notice* your experiences right now (Linehan 1993b). For example, the next time you drink your favorite warm beverage, whether it's hot tea, coffee, cocoa, or something else, really notice and pay attention to how it looks, its color, the way it moves in the cup when you pick it up, its aroma, how it feels in your mouth, the various tastes you experience, and so on. Keep your mind focused right on the present and on your experience of drinking your favorite hot beverage.

The idea is for you to step back in your mind and pay attention to your experience of the present moment, using your senses: sight, hearing, touch, taste, and smell. Pay close attention. If your mind wanders, bring it back again to what you're focusing on. Don't struggle with or try to change or escape from what you're paying attention to. Beyond your five senses, you can also observe your thoughts.

Another way to practice mindfulness is to *label* or put words to your experiences (ibid.). While you are drinking your hot beverage, the idea here would be to describe to yourself what you notice. For example, *The cup feels warm and smooth in my hands, I see steam rising from the cup, The coffee shows ripples on the surface as I pick up the cup, It smells "roasty" and smoky, The taste is of slightly burned toast and chocolate,* and *My mouth feels saturated with warmth.* Use words to describe exactly what you see, hear, smell, taste, touch, or think. Just describe the facts without adding any judgments, inferences, opinions, guesses, or hunches. Don't assume anything. Be really concrete and specific, and stick to the facts.

Another way to practice mindfulness—and in some ways, this is the goal of mindfulness in DBT (Chapman and Linehan 2005)—is to *throw yourself into* or *immerse yourself in* (Linehan 1993b) whatever you are doing in the present moment. With the hot beverage, the idea would be to really immerse yourself in the whole experience of drinking the beverage. Make this the one and only thing you do, and throw your mind and body completely into it. Pay attention to exactly what you're doing, making whatever you are doing right now the most important thing you could possibly do. Do it with vigor and energy, and with your whole mind and body. Finally, in DBT mindfulness skills, as with most other types of mindfulness, there are three important things to always keep in mind (ibid.):

- **Do one thing at a time.** Do only one thing in the moment, one thing at a time. Avoid multitasking; avoid juggling different tasks. Just put your whole mind on this one activity, right here and now, whether that activity is driving, eating, walking, washing the dishes, talking with someone, reading a book, arguing, working, or waiting.

- **Avoid judging.** Don't judge yourself, others, or your experiences. Avoid labeling anything "good," "bad," "right," "wrong," "should," or "should not." If you catch yourself judging, then bring your mind back to the present or describe just the facts. Don't judge yourself for judging, either (ibid.).

- **Do what works.** Learn from your experiences what works to reach your goals, and do the things that work. Don't beat your head against the wall doing things that you want to do or feel like doing but that ultimately don't work for you.

Benefits of DBT Mindfulness Skills

As you can probably see, one major benefit of mindfulness is that if you really practice it, you will spend a lot more time experiencing your life as it is right now, rather than being tormented by anxious or distressing thoughts about your past or future. Mindfulness, then, can be the antidote to some of the distressing thought patterns that people with anxiety often experience.

Next, we list some of the other benefits that you might experience if you practice mindfulness skills, including those specific to anxiety problems as well as more general benefits. Many of the people we have worked with have commented on these benefits, and mindfulness research (Baer 2003) also supports the idea that many people achieve at least some of them.

- You learn to pay attention to your thoughts, emotions, and experiences in the here and now, and learn to see them for what they are.

- You learn to step back and notice your current situation, observe your thoughts and emotions, and decide on a wise course of action.

- Instead of avoiding your emotions at all costs, you can learn to step back and experience them, notice them, and then figure out what to do about them.

- You learn to disengage from worry, rumination, and obsessive thoughts.

- You live a richer, fuller life.

- You enjoy positive experiences more acutely.

- You learn to be more present with other people.

- You understand yourself better and with more clarity.

We hope that as we guide you through the mindfulness skills in this workbook, you'll realize many of these benefits in your daily life and in dealing with anxiety problems.

Exercise 3.1 Get Started with Mindfulness Skills

Here is an exercise in using the skill of noticing or paying attention to your experiences in the here and now, or mindful observation. Here are some important instructions to follow before you get started:

1. Find a quiet place where you can sit without anyone bothering you for about five to ten minutes.

2. Get into a comfortable position, sitting on a couch or chair, the floor, or mats or pillows if you have them.

3. Start paying attention and noticing according to the following instructions (paying attention to sounds, the sensation of sitting, and what you see around you).

4. Remember that if your mind wanders or you feel like moving, scratching an itch, getting up, or stopping the exercise, simply observe these experiences and turn your mind back to what you were paying attention to. Similarly, if you start to get swept up in your thoughts, gently escort your mind back to your focus of attention.

5. Remember that mindfulness is simple but not easy; don't be hard on yourself if you have a difficult time with this exercise or your mind wanders. Minds wander; that's simply what they do. The whole practice of mindfulness is simply bringing your mind back to the present whenever it wanders somewhere else, so if your mind wanders a thousand times, that means you get a thousand times more practice than if it wanders only once. Be sure to try each step of the exercise for a few minutes before you move on to the next one.

Here are the instructions for mindful observation:

1. **Start by paying attention to the sounds that you hear.** Shine the spotlight of your attention on sounds. Listen attentively, carefully, and with curiosity, as if all the sounds you hear were new to you. Just see what you notice.

2. **Bring the spotlight of your attention to the sensations of sitting.** Notice what it feels like to be sitting down, notice where the chair or cushion contacts your body, and pay attention to any sensations, whether you notice pressure, warmth, pain, hardness, or any other sensation. Whatever you notice is perfectly okay; just pay attention.

3. **Now bring your attention to what you see around you.** Start by looking down at the floor, and notice what you see there. If you have emotional reactions to or thoughts about what you see, simply allow them to come and go, and bring your mind back to what you see. Slowly raise your gaze from the floor, and look at the walls and furniture (if you're in a room with walls and furniture). Pay close attention to each object you look at. Try your best to look at it with curiosity, as if you have never seen it before.

As you'll see in later chapters, you can use this skill of simply noticing or observing to pay attention to other things as well, such as your emotions, your thoughts, your breathing, or pretty much anything that is happening right here and now.

Do your best to practice mindfulness skills whenever you can, whether you are walking, working, swimming, on vacation, worrying, or planning—whatever you are doing. You can almost always practice mindfulness no matter what you're doing; you simply have to bring your mind to the here and now, and pay attention.

DBT DISTRESS TOLERANCE SKILLS

Distress tolerance skills in DBT were designed to help people deal with overwhelming emotions, thoughts, and situations temporarily until things change (Linehan 1993b). If you suffer from anxiety problems, you're no stranger to overwhelming emotions. Sometimes it might seem as if the only way to deal with your emotions is to curl up and hide somewhere, to completely avoid all thoughts and situations that make you anxious. As discussed, although such strategies can give you short-term relief, they create problems in the long run.

There are other ways to deal with overwhelming anxiety, stress, and tension—ways that can help you feel a little better in the moment *and* that have long-term benefits. That's what the distress tolerance skills are all about, and they have several benefits for people who struggle with a variety of emotional problems, including those related to anxiety.

Tolerating Distress

Everyone at times has difficulty tolerating distress. That's no surprise, of course; distress is distressing! All things being equal, most people probably would not choose to feel as often as they do such intense negative emotions as severe anxiety, shame, anger, sadness, or guilt. They'd probably choose to not have extremely overwhelming or stressful things happen either, or to experience repeated, upsetting, or unwanted thoughts. But, the fact is that these things do happen, and for many people these experiences can become so overwhelming that they simply don't know what to do.

Distress tolerance skills are designed to help in exactly those moments when you feel overwhelmed and need to do something to ride out an emotional storm until things can change. It's important to remember that distress tolerance skills won't necessarily solve your problems, but they will help you to tolerate or deal with them without making anything worse.

Let's say that you just lost your job; your partner has left you; and you feel unbelievably hurt, anxious, and overwhelmed. Here are some examples of different ways to react. You might notice that you've done some of these things yourself.

- **Ruminate and think it to death.** You could ask yourself why this is happening to you. Really dig deep into your brain and think about why you feel the way you do and why these upsetting things keep happening to you. Run it again and again in your mind until you've turned over every possible leaf and come up with some explanation. Worry and think about all the implications, what might be wrong with you (like that you are unlovable and will never have another partner, or that you're not smart or organized enough to hold a job), and what bad things might happen in the future. If you're familiar with this way of coping, you probably also have noticed that it is one straight path to distress, despair, and agony.

- **Escape at all costs.** Another way to cope is to do your best to simply escape your feelings and your situations at all costs. You might try to avoid all thoughts about your job loss or your breakup; procrastinate and avoid doing anything about it; suppress, clamp down on, or get rid of any emotions that pop up; or use alcohol, drugs, self-harm, binge eating, or other coping methods to escape your feelings and get some relief. If you've done this—and many people have, from time to time—you might have noticed that this way of dealing with things not only doesn't solve your problems but also creates more problems.

- **Use distress tolerance skills.** Finally, another way to deal with an overwhelming situation is to practice tolerating your emotions, your thoughts, and the situation itself. For instance, you might temporarily distract yourself from overwhelming emotions and thoughts by spending time with others, getting involved in an activity that grabs your attention, or doing physical exercise or something else, until you feel calmer and better able to think and plan. You could also soothe yourself by doing something calming, such as listening to relaxing music, doing artwork, or taking a warm bath. You also could try not to struggle with your emotions or thoughts; accept them, letting them come and go; remind yourself that your reactions are understandable; and do your best to accept (at least for now) that you are in an incredibly upsetting situation.

This third way of coping is exactly what the distress tolerance skills are all about. It may not sound easy to do these things, but with practice, it gets easier.

The Basics of DBT Distress Tolerance Skills

There are two types of DBT distress tolerance skills. One type involves learning to ride out a crisis or overwhelming situation without making anything worse, until you can do something about your situation. These skills are called *crisis survival skills*. The second type of distress tolerance skills is called *reality acceptance skills*, and they involve learning to accept your situation for what it is right now in the present.

REALITY ACCEPTANCE SKILLS

One way to tolerate distressful, upsetting, or overwhelming situations is to practice accepting things exactly the way they are (Linehan 1993b). To do this, try your best to let go of your struggle to change your thoughts, emotions, or the situation right now in the present moment and to allow things to be exactly as they are.

This sounds kind of strange, doesn't it? If you are paralyzed with fear about leaving your home or being in company, or are tormented by worries, why would you want to let go of the struggle to change things? Why on earth would you want to accept things the way they are? Well, paradoxically, many people we have worked with have found that accepting things just the way they are, at least for right now, has often been the only way out of their suffering. Also, acceptance is the antidote to emotional avoidance, and many people have found that acceptance can be a life-changing, new way to relate to their own experiences.

By "accept," we don't mean surrender, give up, or even like or enjoy your experiences; we simply mean stopping the constant struggle to run away or escape from your experiences and allowing them to be what they are. You can accept something and still work to change it. In fact, to successfully change something in your life, you may need to accept it first. For instance, you can accept that you struggle with an anxiety disorder, and doing so might make you feel more at peace with yourself and less judgmental about your problems. At the same time, you can read this book and seek therapy or treatment to help yourself change.

Another important point about acceptance is that you do not need to accept the future. We know that you can accept the past because the past has already happened, and realistically what else are you going to do? It also makes a lot of sense to accept the present, because it is happening. But, you can't know exactly what will happen in the future, so we would suggest that you be careful about accepting what might or might not occur in the future. If it helps you to accept things about the future, make sure that those things you choose to accept are very likely to happen. Otherwise, acceptance can easily lead to hopelessness about the future (*I have to accept that I'll never have a job or a romantic partner, make decent money, be happy, be less anxious,* and so on).

Here are a few other important points about acceptance:

- Acceptance is something you continually practice but never complete. Acceptance can be a lifelong practice; it's not like passing a test or finishing a course.

- Acceptance gets easier and more effective the more you practice it.

- Acceptance does not get rid of your emotions or thoughts; it helps you to have them without as much suffering.

- Don't use acceptance to avoid your emotions, thoughts, or life.

- Acceptance can feel invalidating (that is, dismissive of the gravity of your problems) if someone else tells you to do it ("Just accept it!"). Don't let that stop you, and don't use it in an invalidating way with yourself. Just encourage yourself to drop the struggle against reality, and practice allowing things to be the way they are right now (but not necessarily forever).

Acceptance also can help you to allow things to be the way they are and to do what is effective or needed. Often, people resentfully refuse to accept things the way they are or even to do anything that might help their situation (because they don't want it to be the way it is in the first place). Dr. Marsha Linehan (1993b) calls this *willfulness*, which involves railing against reality, refusing to accept things the way they are, pretending that things are different or acting as if things were not the way they are, trying to force things to be different, and refusing to do what is effective or required (ibid.).

Let's say, for example, that your boss uses an incredibly blunt manner when giving you feedback on your performance, and you and your coworkers have found that this is not going to change anytime soon. You feel hurt and angry when your boss gives you feedback in this way, and you don't want to accept it. In fact, you keep saying to yourself, *My boss shouldn't be this way! This is not appropriate!* Then, feeling angry, you refuse to accept the feedback from your boss (even if the delivery is poor but the message is valid) or to do anything to help yourself cope with your emotional reactions to that feedback, because you think, *This shouldn't be happening in the first place.* Therefore, you just end up more upset and, during the next performance review, get the same feedback in the same annoying manner, because you haven't changed anything. This would be an example of willfulness.

In contrast, if you were practicing acceptance, you could work on accepting that your boss has this unfortunate interpersonal style and that it hurts you, and then figuring out what to do about it. For instance, you might use an emotion regulation skill (see the next chapter) to deal with your hurt feelings, use mindfulness to allow the comments to roll off your back, or start looking for a different job with a boss whose style is more compatible with your needs.

Finally, when you practice acceptance, it often helps to make a commitment to yourself in the moment to take that path. Sometimes, when difficult things happen, it's as if you have reached a fork in the road, and on one path (let's call it the "Path to Misery"), you have avoidance, denial, worry, rumination, willfulness, and all the things you could do that lead to more suffering. On the other path, the road leads to acceptance, where you might still have upsetting thoughts or emotions but are able to come to some kind of peace with them. Do your best to remind yourself, whenever you need to, to take this latter path, toward acceptance.

• *Jane's Story*

Struggling with chronic anxiety, tension, and worry, Jane took medications (anxiety-reducing medications called *benzodiazepines*) several times a day to reduce her feelings of tension and anxiety. In addition to these issues, she had recently been sexually assaulted, had memories of past sexual abuse by her father, and experienced periodic episodes of depression lasting several weeks. She was making a lot of progress in therapy, and she really needed support and help to get through all of her difficulties. But, when her therapist moved to another office, Jane became paralyzed with a fear of taking public transportation. She worried that she would misread the bus or train schedule and show up late, that people would look at her on the bus and know that she was going to therapy, that she would have to talk to people and wouldn't know what to say, or that she would take the wrong bus.

Jane started to resent her therapist for moving to a different office, and she tried to convince her to rent an office closer to her home or to see her in a local coffee shop or a similar venue. This became a big topic of discussion during each session, even while Jane was tortured by some of her other problems, which she couldn't address while remaining so focused on this anxiety. After a few weeks, Jane and her therapist realized that despite their efforts to go through anxiety-reduction strategies, deal with Jane's worries and fears, and so on, they both had to learn to accept that Jane would likely continue to feel anxious and afraid during her commute. Jane had to learn to allow herself to have the anxiety rather than try desperately to get rid of it. Once she began to do this, she didn't necessarily feel joyous about taking the bus, but she did make her way onto the bus and stop feeling resentful, and over time her anxiety diminished because many of the things she had been afraid of (like being late or bumbling through social interactions) did not actually come true.

CRISIS SURVIVAL SKILLS

In DBT, there are a few skills to help you ride out, or get through, a crisis or emotional storm (Linehan 1993b). Some of the most fundamental tools for dealing with overwhelming distress are *self-soothing* or relaxation strategies. One of the most difficult things to tolerate about anxiety and other emotions are the physiological experiences that go along with them: increased heart rate; feelings of muscle tension; having butterflies in the stomach; feeling flushed, too hot, or too cold; or other such experiences. In DBT distress tolerance skills, as you will learn throughout this book, you are taught strategies to physiologically soothe yourself and calm your body down so that your anxiety is a little more manageable. These strategies may not eliminate anxiety or other emotions, but they can make them less intense and help you get to the point where you can think and make effective decisions about how to deal with your problems.

Another way to deal with overwhelming distress is to *distract* yourself, at least temporarily. Distraction involves doing something that temporarily gets your mind off whatever is upsetting you. We've already written at length about the problems with avoiding your problems, and it might sound as if distraction were just another way to avoid your problems. If you're thinking this, you're correct. The important points here, however, are that distraction has been found in research to be an effective way to cope with emotional distress, and you are to use distraction temporarily, not to distract your entire life away. Another very important point is that for distraction to work, you have to do it mindfully. Pay close attention and throw yourself into whatever activity you are using to distract yourself. If you engage in distracting activities but think about your problems the whole time, then it won't work.

Distraction could involve any activity that temporarily gets your mind focused on something other than whatever is bothering you. A few examples of distraction strategies often used in DBT are (ibid.):

- Engaging in activities that focus your mind on something other than your problems. Examples include spending time with people; going for a walk or exercising; getting out of your immediate environment and going somewhere else; doing arts, crafts, or hobbies; getting some work or studying done; and eating (not too much or too little). The trick is to do activities that really grab your attention and give your brain some temporary relief from your problems.

- Doing something that helps other people, organizations, animals, or the world. Really throwing yourself into helping activities can draw your attention away from your problems and make you feel a sense of self-respect. Examples include cooking a nice meal for someone, contributing to a charity, helping someone get across the street, smiling and being extra friendly to people you see in public, and calling up a friend who you know needs support.

- Another way to use distraction is to get your mind busy. For example, you might subtract from 684 by 7s until you get to 5 (assuming that you don't have a problem with compulsive counting); do a crossword, sudoku, or other type of puzzle; work on a demanding or challenging project; or play video games.

Benefits of DBT Distress Tolerance Skills

There are many benefits to distress tolerance skills for people who suffer from anxiety problems, people who are dealing with other psychological or emotional difficulties, and people without any psychological disorders. Indeed, most everyone could stand to benefit from a little practice with distress tolerance skills. Here are some of the main benefits you might notice if you practice these skills. We hope that as you go through this book, you notice these and other benefits, particularly those that help you with anxiety problems.

- You accept pain in life and experience less suffering.

- You feel more at peace with your problems, even as you work to change them.

- You learn to tolerate previously intolerable emotions or thoughts.

- You become disentangled from distressful thinking patterns, such as worry and rumination.

- You avoid making things worse.

- You feel free of the need to always have to fix or change things right now.

Exercise 3.2 Get Started with Distress Tolerance Skills

This exercise uses the skill of accepting things as they are. Find a quiet place where you will not be bothered; get into a comfortable sitting position; and if your mind wanders during the exercise, just do your best to gently guide it back to what you're focusing on. We suggest that you do this exercise with your eyes closed.

1. Start by thinking of something (whether it's a thought, emotion, or current or past situation in your life) that you have a moderate amount of difficulty accepting. You can think of acceptance as being on a scale from 0 (*I couldn't stand or accept this for even a minute*) to 100 (*I could stand or accept this for a hundred years*). Choose something that's approximately in the middle, around 50 or so. Think of that thing. Write down the number that represents how much you accept this particular thing.

2. Next, tense up your muscles, and fold your arms over your chest. Really try to get some muscle tension going in your shoulders, arms, and neck. Scrunch up your face and furrow your brow, making an irritated or angry expression. Tense your facial muscles. Now, think of that thing you're having a hard time accepting, really getting it into your mind. Keep it in your mind, noticing any thoughts or images about it that float through your mind. Stay that way for about one to two minutes, and then note your level of acceptance from 0 to 100.

3. Next, relax your body and facial muscles. Open your arms and rest your hands palms up on your knees or the armrests of your chair or sofa (the "willing hands" strategy from Linehan 1993b). Sit with your legs slightly apart in an open posture. Try to let go of any muscle tension in your shoulders, arms, or neck, or anywhere else in your body. Then, put a very slight smile on your face, just turning up the corners of your mouth very slightly (this is the "half-smile technique" from Linehan 1993b), much like the type of smile seen on the Mona Lisa, the Buddha, or anyone else you've seen who looks serene and at peace. Then, bring that thing that is difficult to accept back into your mind again. Notice any thoughts or images that pop up, and just let them roll in and out of your mind. Stick with the thing you're having difficulty accepting, and keep it in your mind while maintaining your posture and half smile. Note your level of acceptance on a scale from 0 to 100.

4. Notice any difference in your acceptance level, from when you began, to when you had an angry or tense posture, to when you had the more open, relaxed posture with the half smile. Many people notice

that with the more open posture, they find themselves feeling considerably more accepting. Simply changing your bodily posture or muscle tension can change your neurochemistry and brain activity and modulate your emotional reactions, making you feel just a bit more serene and calm. Other people, however, find that this strategy does not change their level of acceptance. The trick with all of these skills is to try them and then use the ones that work best for you.

MOVING FORWARD

So far in this workbook, you've hopefully gotten a clearer understanding of your problems with anxiety, a general idea of what is involved in DBT, and an introduction to two of the major DBT skills (mindfulness and distress tolerance). We put mindfulness and distress tolerance skills together in this chapter, because both of these skills involve your learning to focus on the present moment and accept things the way they are, at least for now. These are fundamental skills, whether you're dealing with anxiety or other problems. Here are some recommendations for you as you move forward with these skills:

- Spend a week or so practicing mindfulness and distress tolerance regularly.

- Look at your calendar, and set a schedule for practicing the skills.

- Try to spend at least five to ten minutes a day practicing mindfulness, acceptance, or another distress tolerance skill (such as self-soothing or distraction). The more you regularly practice these skills, the more they will become habit and easier to put into action when you are experiencing anxiety and stress.

- When you begin, practice these skills to deal with problems that are mild to moderate. Don't try them for the first time with an extremely distressing problem that you've been struggling with for ages. You will get there, but just give yourself a break the first few times you try new skills.

- Note which skills seem to work best for you.

Now that you have a little practice in mindfulness and distress tolerance, in chapter 4 we will go on to discuss two other important sets of DBT skills that we believe you will find extremely helpful: emotion regulation and interpersonal effectiveness.

CHAPTER 4

DBT Emotion Regulation and Interpersonal Effectiveness Skills

Remember in chapter 2, when we talked about how it can be helpful to strike a balance between trying to change yourself and your situation and accepting yourself and your situation as is? Well, in chapter 3, we went through DBT skills that can help you accept things as they are in the moment and combat avoidance. In this chapter, we balance things out a bit by guiding you through some skills to help you change things, specifically strategies to help you change and manage your emotions (emotion regulation skills), as well as your relationships and interactions (interpersonal effectiveness skills).

DBT EMOTION REGULATION SKILLS AND EMOTIONS

One important set of skills taught in DBT is emotion regulation skills. These skills can help you improve the way you manage or regulate your emotions. Researchers have defined *emotion regulation* as the ways in which people influence their emotional states, and how they experience and express their emotions (Gross 1998). Many professionals perceive that problems with emotion regulation are a common thread across many emotional problems and disorders. People with depression, anxiety disorders, substance-use problems, personality disorders, and "psychotic disorders" (schizophrenia, for example) all have at least some difficulties with the management of their emotions. Emotion regulation skills also can be tremendously useful even if you don't have any specific emotional disorder. Who among us couldn't use some helpful hints on how to deal with our emotions more effectively?

To effectively manage your emotions, you need to know exactly what you're dealing with in the first place: what are emotions anyway? Well, scientists who study emotions believe that they are a set of reactions in the body and brain to events, memories, and thoughts (ibid.). Emotional reactions have many different parts, so to speak, much as the mythical beast the hydra has many heads. In DBT, we emphasize the fact that emotions do have many parts to them and that they all work together as one big system, involving your brain, your body, your thoughts, and your actions (Linehan 1993b).

Emotions and Your Brain

Your brain is heavily involved in your emotions. When you feel an emotion, there are changes in your brain and neurochemistry. For instance, when you experience an emotional reaction, one area in your brain that becomes very active is called the *amygdala*, an area in the limbic system involved in motivation, emotions, pleasure, and memory, among other things. You can think of the amygdala as the emotional engine of the brain. It gets really revved up when something triggers an emotional reaction.

Another important area in the brain to know about is the *prefrontal cortex*. An area just behind and above your eyes, it is involved in thinking, planning, decision making, curbing impulses, processing information, and solving problems, among many other functions. If the amygdala is like the emotional engine that revs when you put your foot on the gas, areas of the prefrontal cortex are much like the brakes; they help slow down activity in the amygdala, bringing your emotional state back to a baseline or normal level.

Yet another area of your brain, the *hippocampus* (also in the limbic system) is involved in learning and memory formation. When it comes to emotions, the hippocampus helps you form the memories you need in order to learn from emotional events.

Of course, many other areas of your brain become active when emotions are on the scene, but we highlight these three areas because they are especially involved in emotion regulation. Often, when we talk about emotion regulation, we are talking about your brain learning from your emotional experiences (which the hippocampus helps you with), or putting the brakes (your prefrontal cortex) on emotional reactions that are not working for you.

As an example, let's say that you were angry with your boss because it had been quite some time since you received a raise. When you brought this up with your boss, you raised your voice, and then you got reprimanded and felt embarrassed. Well, your amygdala probably was quite active when you felt angry with your boss, and when you raised your voice, your prefrontal cortex was probably trying its best to slow down and reduce your emotional reactions to get you to think things through (unfortunately, in this case, it failed). When your boss reprimanded you and you felt embarrassed, again your amygdala was probably active, and then your hippocampus likely kicked in so that your brain remembered, *It's not such a great idea to yell at your boss!*

Emotions and Your Body

Another aspect of your emotions has to do with the changes in your body that occur when you have an emotion (Linehan 1993b). Many bodily changes occur when you experience an emotion: changes in heart rate, body temperature, muscle tension, and the activities of your sweat glands, hormones, tear ducts, and other physical functions.

Think of the last time you felt extremely angry. Then, use exercise 4.1 to write down all the changes that happened in your body when you felt angry. Did you feel increases in muscle tension? Did your heart rate seem to change by increasing, decreasing, or pounding? Did you notice any changes in your face—for instance, a flushing sensation?

Exercise 4.1 Physical Signs of Emotions

Use this table to get familiar with the physical signs of different emotions you might experience. Start with anger, and then try out other emotions, including both positive and negative ones. For now, until you get the hang of it, try to focus on emotions other than anxiety. Later, we will talk about how all of these skills apply to anxiety. For now, though, just think about other emotions.

First, under "Emotion Name and Intensity," name your emotion (like anger, sadness, calmness, happiness, guilt, and so on), and then rate how intense it was from 0 (no emotion at all) to 10 (most intense that you have ever felt). Then, in the "Muscles" column, briefly describe what you felt in your muscles. Were they tense? Did they feel heavy, tired, twitchy, or relaxed? Next, in the "Heart Rate" column, briefly describe whether your heart rate increased or decreased or you experienced your heart pounding in your chest. In the "Body Temperature" column, do the same thing for body temperature: Did it increase or decrease? Did you feel perspiration, warmth or coldness, or some other sensation? Finally, you can use the "Other" column to describe other physical experiences that accompanied the emotion. There is room at the bottom of the form for you to add any additional information that may be helpful to you. We provided an example of anger, but you may also describe your own experience of anger, if different

Emotion Name and Intensity	Muscles	Heart Rate	Body Temperature	Other
Anger	Tense neck, shoulders	Pounding heart, quicker heartbeat	Hot in my neck/face, cool feet	Feeling of adrenaline surge in chest
Comments:				

Emotions can also occasion changes in your posture or facial expressions or the speed of your movements. When you've felt really sad, have you ever noticed your limbs feel heavy, your movements and rate of speech slow down, or your tone of voice and facial expressions change? In contrast, think of how your face looks, how you speak, and how your body acts when you feel very angry. Different emotions often mean different bodily sensations, as well as differences in facial expressions, tone of voice, and other factors. Often, it is because of these changes that we know we are experiencing an emotion in the first place. Also, one of the best ways to change an emotion is simply to change your bodily movements, posture, or facial expression. In fact, research studies have found that the muscles that move when you change your facial expression—for example, by smiling—trigger a host of changes in your neurochemistry (LeDoux 1996). These changes can then modify how you feel (Soussignan 2002).

Emotions and Your Thoughts

Another component of emotions has to do with the thoughts that you have when you feel certain emotions. You can think of these thoughts as passengers coming along for the ride on the emotions bus (Hayes and Smith 2005). In contrast to emotions (which have to do with what you feel), thoughts are the things you say to yourself or the images you picture in your mind. For instance, *Things are hopeless* is a thought that might go along with a feeling of sadness or despair. Thoughts have to do with what you are saying about a situation, an emotion, yourself, or other people. And, different thoughts often go along with different emotions. Next, we list some of the types of thinking patterns that might accompany different emotional states. Although this is far from an exhaustive list, it will help give you a sense of some of the thoughts that often go along with certain emotions. Of course, it is important to keep in mind that you may have other thoughts or different kinds of thoughts that go along with these emotions for you. These are just examples.

- Thoughts that go along with anger might include *I can't stand him! Why is he always like this? What a jerk. She should never have said that! This is awful. How dare they do this to me? This should not be happening like this!*

- Thoughts that go along with guilt might include *I should never have done what I did. I really hurt her. I need to make up for this. I don't know why I keep doing these things.*

- Thoughts that go along with sadness might include *This is so awful. What am I going to do? I can't believe this is happening. I'm going to miss this person so much.*

A very important point to remember about thoughts is that they can both fuel your emotions and be fueled by your emotions. Sometimes, you get angry only after you have a bunch of angry thoughts, and at other times you might find that you get angry and then that feeling of anger sets you down the road of having a bunch of angry thoughts. Or, you might find that they all come at once in a big bundle of anger. There's a back-and-forth relationship between thoughts and emotions; thus, you can change your thoughts by changing your emotions, and you can change your emotions by changing your thoughts. This is not, however, to say that if you have strong emotions, the problem is in your head. We're not saying that thoughts are the main or only cause of emotional distress, or that all you have to do is change your thinking and everything will be fine. Thoughts play a role sometimes, but they are just one part of the picture.

Exercise 4.2 Relating Your Emotions to Your Thoughts

Using this table, write down different types of emotions that you experience, including both positive and negative emotions, and then note the types of thoughts that go through your mind when you feel these particular emotions. There is an example in the table to get you started.

Emotion Name	Thoughts
Anger	*She shouldn't have said that; this is wrong; I hate this; why does this keep happening? What a pain! I can't stand this! He is such a jerk.*

Emotions and Your Actions

Finally, yet another aspect of emotions is your behavior or the things you do when you feel certain emotions. In fact, many scientists believe that emotions were put on this earth to help animals take action and do things to promote their own survival. For instance, the emotion of fear helps motivate you to avoid dangerous things, like poisonous snakes, lions, and bears. The problem, of course, is that many of the things humans are afraid of now (like public speaking, garter snakes, going outside, or feeling negative emotions) are not likely to kill us. But, fear still does have great survival value even now. If you didn't feel any fear, for instance, you might not move fast enough to get out of the way of a truck barreling toward you as you cross the street.

Most of the other emotions also help us in many ways, even if we are not always aware of this. Sadness when you lose someone or something important to you can help you to take the time you need to soothe and care for yourself, and it can also (if you express sadness to others) get you some help and social support. Anger can motivate you to take action and change harmful situations. For instance, if the folks in Parkersburg, West Virginia, had not felt indignant or angry about the pollution of their drinking water from a huge factory nearby, they probably wouldn't have taken any action (which resulted in a class-action lawsuit and the cleaning up of the water system), and they would still be sipping Teflon-related compounds with their morning coffee.

As you learn about emotion regulation skills in this chapter and in others, it's important to remember four very important points (we reiterate here some of the important points Dr. Marsha Linehan made in her 2007 video *Opposite Action: Changing Emotions You Want to Change*):

- Different emotions come along with different action tendencies.

- If you change your actions, you can change your emotions.

- Emotion regulation is all about changing your behavior, your actions, and, in some cases, your thoughts.

- You can't change your emotions by sheer force of will (if you could, you probably wouldn't be reading this book, and we probably wouldn't be writing it!).

Exercise 4.3 Relating Emotions to Your Actions

Using this table, write down different types of emotions that you experience, including both positive and negative emotions, and note the types of actions that often go along with these different emotions. There is an example in the table to get you started.

Emotion Name	Thoughts
Anger	*Irritated voice tone, yelling, moving quickly, clenching fists, talking quickly and loudly*

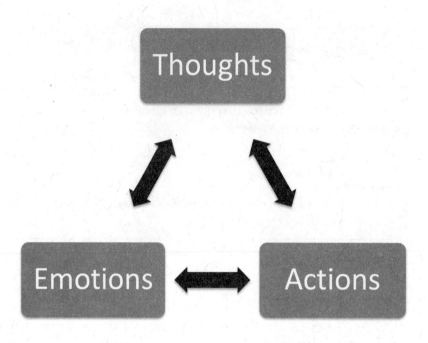

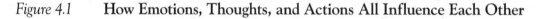

Figure 4.1   **How Emotions, Thoughts, and Actions All Influence Each Other**

THE BASICS OF DBT EMOTION REGULATION SKILLS

As we mentioned, emotion regulation has to do with the ways in which people influence which emotions they have, when they have them, and how they experience and express their emotions (Gross 1998). The DBT emotion regulation skills help you manage your emotions in three primary ways. First, there are skills that help you learn to identify and understand your emotions (Linehan 1993b). If you learn to understand and identify your emotions, you might find that they feel more manageable and less distressing and frightening. Second, there are skills to help you reduce your vulnerability to negative or unwanted emotions. Often, these skills involve improving your own physical and emotional self-care, engaging in positive activities, and doing things that make you feel confident and capable (ibid.). Third, there are skills to help you change and manage your emotions. Some of these skills involve learning to step back from, notice, and pay attention to your emotions without escaping from or struggling with them. Other skills involve learning to act in a way that goes against the grain of, or opposes, what you feel like doing when you experience an emotion (ibid.). In future chapters, we will help you use these skills to deal with anxiety and its problems specifically.

Benefits of DBT Emotion Regulation Skills

As you have probably noticed, we all have to regulate or manage our emotions on a daily basis to get our needs met and achieve our goals. If you never did anything to manage your emotions, you probably wouldn't be able to do many of the things that are important to you. For example, if we felt stressed out and anxious about all of the writing we had to do to finish this book, and we simply did what those emotions told us to do (for example, turn off the computer, avoid work, put off the writing), then you probably wouldn't be reading these words right now. We often have to regulate or manage (or at the very least, notice) our emotions in order to get through the day and to deal with people.

Have you ever been in a situation in which someone close to you kept doing something that bothered you, and you felt irritated about it but didn't really recognize that you were irritated or do anything to manage your irritation? What happened? Well, if you're like a lot of people, that irritation probably continued to build until you eventually exploded or said something you later regretted. If, instead, you had managed to catch these feelings when they were less intense and then had either managed these feelings for yourself or tried to get the person to change, things might have gone differently. So, in short, there are many, many benefits to learning how to effectively manage your emotions. Here are just a few, but we hope that you notice others as you go through this book.

Getting Started with Emotion Regulation Skills

Here is an exercise to get you started with some emotion regulation skills. As with the mindfulness skills, try to find a quiet place where you can work on them without anyone bothering you for fifteen to twenty minutes. We have included just one of the different ways to practice emotion regulation skills here, but there are several more in the specific chapters ahead.

This exercise has to do with understanding and identifying your emotions. This is the most important first step in learning how to manage or regulate your emotions. Therefore, next, we walk you through the steps to begin to understand three aspects of your emotions: physical sensations, action urges, and thoughts. Once you have practiced this skill of simply stepping back and noticing your emotions, you will be better prepared to use some of the strategies for managing your emotions that we talk about in other chapters.

Exercise 4.4 Physical Sensations, Action Urges, and Thoughts

Be sure to do this exercise when you feel an emotion, either positive (joy, happiness) or negative (anger or sadness), at least at a moderate intensity (like 5 out of a possible 10, where 0 means no emotion at all, and 10 means the strongest emotion you've ever felt).

1. **Physical sensations:** Sit down and pay attention to how you feel. Using the skill of mindful noticing mentioned previously, start by paying attention to the sensations you experience in your body. Do you notice anything about your heart rate or body temperature? Do your muscles feel tense or relaxed? What about any sensations in your belly, shoulders, head, neck, back, or other areas? Pay attention to where in your body you feel the emotion. Once you have observed for a couple of minutes, take a piece of paper and write down "Physical Sensations," and then note the physical sensations that you just noticed.

2. **Action urges:** Next, notice any desires or urges you have to do anything. These are called "action urges." Often, action urges come along with emotions, because the point of an emotion is often to get you to do something. For instance, anger makes you want to attack or get rid of what is making you

angry. So, for this part of the exercise, just sit and notice any urges to do anything. Do you feel like getting away from or escaping your emotions? Do you feel like yelling at someone? Do you feel like getting up and running; or crawling under the covers and sleeping, hiding, or doing nothing? Just notice what you feel like doing, and then write it down.

3. **Thoughts:** Finally, notice the thoughts that are going through your mind. What are you saying to yourself? What thoughts or images are passing across your mind? Thoughts often go along with emotions. Sometimes thoughts trigger emotions, and sometimes emotions trigger thoughts. Simply notice the thoughts you are experiencing. Thoughts are different from emotions, in that they often come in the form of words or images, whereas emotions are more like experiences that you sense in your body, such as muscle tension or other experiences you may have noticed previously. Simply notice whatever thoughts are going through your mind. It doesn't matter what they are; just pay attention to them until you have a clear idea of what you're thinking and then write it down.

Excellent! Now, you have a great start on DBT emotion regulation skills. As we mentioned, the remaining chapters of this book will walk you step by step through how to use these skills to help you with your anxiety.

DBT INTERPERSONAL EFFECTIVENESS SKILLS

Finally, another important set of skills taught in DBT is *interpersonal effectiveness (IE) skills*. These skills help you interact more effectively. Often, the greatest feelings of joy, misery, disappointment, excitement, and anxiety all occur in the context of interpersonal relationships. And, people with anxiety problems often worry about and have difficulties in their interactions. As a result, they might avoid people or even avoid leaving their homes altogether for fear of encountering others.

Often, interpersonal problems can make anxiety and other emotional problems worse. In the same way, emotional or anxiety problems can make interpersonal problems worse. For example, if you suffer from social anxiety disorder, you likely avoid situations where you need to talk, eat, or do other such activities in front of people. You might also avoid being assertive with others, asking for what you want, or saying no to things people ask you to do. Now, the problem with this is that the more you avoid these types of situations, the harder it is to manage them in the future and the more you miss out on opportunities to learn how to negotiate challenging interpersonal situations.

Basically, the more you avoid, the more you miss out on the chance to learn new skills and overcome interpersonal problems. In addition, even if you have learned these skills before or used them in the past, you might find that you need a refresher in interpersonal skills, because you have been avoiding people for so long that your skills have become weaker, much like a muscle that hasn't been used for a while. If you were a pilot who hasn't flown for many years, you would probably want a refresher course on how to fly a plane before you got into the cockpit again (or at least, as frequent flyers, we'd hope you would take some kind of refresher course).

In the end, even if you do your best to stop avoiding interpersonal situations, you might find that you don't have all of the tools necessary to navigate your relationships, which may make you more likely to avoid again. Now, just as we mentioned when we talked about DBT emotion regulation skills, interpersonal skills can be helpful for people with a variety of difficulties, as well as people in general. Any of us could benefit from sharpening our interpersonal skills and improving the ways in which we interact with others. That's what IE skills are all about. More specifically, through DBT interpersonal effectiveness skills, you learn how to be assertive by effectively asking for what you want from others, saying no to unwanted requests, balancing your priorities in relationships, and keeping an eye on your goals in relationships (Linehan 1993b).

Interpersonal Problems to Work On

There are all kinds of interpersonal problems that people can have. In this section, we talk about some of the main types of problems that the DBT interpersonal effectiveness skills address. As you read through this section, think about whether (and when) you struggle with these particular difficulties.

DIFFICULTY ASKING PEOPLE FOR THINGS OR SAYING NO

Some people have tremendous difficulty asking others for things they want, whether they want something tangible, like an object or money, or something less tangible, like help or support. As a result, they might avoid asking altogether (Linehan 1993b). If you are a person who doesn't ask for what you want, think about the types of problems that may come up for you because of this.

Let's say that you live with someone who rarely cleans up after herself or himself. The first time it happens, you feel irritated and frustrated, but you just go ahead and clean up after this person, hoping that things will change. Over time, however, you notice that this keeps happening, and you keep feeling irritated and frustrated. But, you never bring it up or ask the person to change. What do you think might happen? Well, you will probably feel a growing resentment about all the work you're doing. You might also start to feel irritated with this person at other times (even when you're having a nice time together). And, eventually things might just blow up one day. This is the problem with not asking people for things you need or changes that are important to you: the problems mount and begin to sour the relationship.

Similarly, you might be a person who has a hard time saying no to things. Well, if this is the case, the same problems can happen as described previously. You might find that you keep saying yes to things you don't really want to do or even to things that go against your values. Then, you might end up feeling overwhelmed, taken advantage of, or resentful, and your own self-respect might begin to erode (ibid.).

DIFFICULTY KNOWING HOW STRONGLY OR INTENSELY TO ASK, OR HOW TO SAY NO

Many people also have difficulty determining how intensely to ask for something or say no to a request (Linehan 1993b). For example, there may be times when you ask people for what you want in too subtle or tentative of a manner to be taken seriously. At other times, however, you might say things too strongly or aggressively. The challenge here is to ask people for things in a way that is appropriate for the situation. If you are in a burning building and a large man is blocking the doorway to the only way out, the best option is probably to yell, "Move!" Quietly hinting (gesturing with your head toward the fire and the escape door) or saying, "Excuse me, would you mind moving?" is probably not the most effective course of action. On the other hand, if you ask your boss for a raise, you will probably encounter some trouble if you take the same approach as you do with the person blocking the burning building's escape route.

Over the long run, if you are always really intense in how you ask for things or even in how you say no to things in close relationships, you might find that people tend to burn out. If, however, you always ask or say no in a very timid and tentative manner, or rely on indirect requests and hints, you may not get your needs met, or you might end up frustrated that people don't seem to understand what you need. The bottom line is that in relationships, it is important to know how strongly to make requests or say no to things: you want to be appropriately assertive rather than either too passive or timid, or too aggressive.

Exercise 4.5 Self-Assessment: Where Do You Need Help with Interpersonal Skills?

Please answer these questions to determine where you need the most help with your IE skills. Then, add up your total score in each of the following categories.

1 = strongly disagree; 2 = disagree; 3 = neutral; 4 = agree; 5 = strongly agree.	
Difficulty Making Requests	**Score**
1. I'm afraid people won't like me if I ask them to change what they do.	
2. I often wait until something is really bothering me before saying anything.	
3. I have difficulty asking people for help.	
4. I don't know how to ask people for what I want.	
Total	
Difficulty Saying No	**Score**
1. I'm afraid people won't like me if I say no.	
2. I often say yes to things I don't want to do.	
3. I often do things for people that go against my morals or values.	
4. I frequently get overwhelmed by all the things I do for other people.	
Total	

Too Intense	Score
1. I often demand that others do what I want.	
2. I frequently yell, raise my voice, or use strong language to get what I want.	
3. If people say no to me, I keep asking until they say yes.	
4. When I say no, I often refuse adamantly, and I don't budge.	
Total	
Not Intense Enough	Score
1. When I want to ask people for things, I hint or avoid asking altogether.	
2. I expect others to know what I want.	
3. I am often frustrated, because others don't seem to get my hints.	
4. I am fairly timid or tentative when I ask for things or say no to requests.	
Total	
If you find that you scored above 12 on some of these scales, then those are the ones you might need to focus on as you build your IE skills.	

The Basics of DBT Interpersonal Effectiveness Skills

The IE skills in DBT teach you how to ask for what you need or say no to others' requests in an effective way, as well as how to navigate your interactions with others in a way that is consistent with your values and goals. You are taught a few main things in IE skills. First, you are taught to identify your goals in terms of an interaction. Second, you are taught how to ask for things, say no, or express your opinion in an appropriate and effective manner. Third, you are taught how strongly or intensely to ask, say no, or assert your opinion.

IDENTIFYING YOUR GOALS AND NEEDS

When you interact with others, it can be very helpful to figure out what you want out of the interaction, or your goals and needs. Otherwise, you might lose sight of what you want from the relationship or interaction, or you might not do things that get you closer to your goals. In DBT interpersonal effectiveness skills, we talk about goals in three different areas (Linehan 1993b): what you want out of the situation, how you want to affect your relationship or how the other person feels about you, and how you want to feel about yourself during and after the interaction. Each of these goals is often very important. For instance, you might want your boss to give you a raise, but if your relationship with your boss is on the rocks, you might lose your job. So, before you ask for a raise, you might want to think about how you want your boss to feel about you and the relationship. In addition, you might really want a raise, but if you have to beg and plead on your knees in order to get it, you might feel bad about yourself or lose some self-respect. Therefore, it's important to think about how you want to feel about yourself as a result of the interaction with your boss.

At the start of every interpersonal interaction, it can be helpful to think about what you want from the situation in each of these areas: clarify your goals. Although your goals in all three areas are usually important, take some time to think about which of the previously mentioned goals are the most important, as this will determine your approach.

ASKING, STATING AN OPINION, OR SAYING NO

In DBT interpersonal effectiveness skills (Linehan 1993b), you are taught several primary steps to take to effectively state your opinion, ask for something, or say no to something:

1. Explain the situation to the other person clearly and objectively so that the person knows exactly what the issue is.

2. Let the person know how you feel about the situation using "I feel" and "I think" statements.

3. State your needs and what you want out of the situation as specifically as possible.

4. Clarify up front how this will benefit the other person.

5. Identify ahead of time (just in case you need them) any compromises you might be willing to make to get your needs met (ibid.).

In addition, it is important to make sure that you say all of this in a way that meets your relationship goals, and in a way that doesn't compromise your values or make you feel bad about yourself.

Let's say that the situation is that your partner's job is to do the dishes, and you often come home from a long, hard day of work to find that the dishes are not done. Here is an example of how you might use these skills to communicate your needs regarding the dishes:

1. "I have noticed that the dishes are often not done when I get home from my late-evening shift on Thursdays" (explaining the situation).

2. "And I feel overwhelmed when I get home late and have to clean up the kitchen" (letting the person know how you feel about the situation).

3. "Please take some time early in the evening to clear the dishes from dinner" (stating your needs and asking for what you want).

4. "If you could do this for me, I would be so much less stressed out" (clarifying how this will benefit the other person).

5. "And maybe I could help you by cleaning up on Tuesdays in return" (stating a compromise you'd be willing to make).

We have a few tips about this way of communicating. First, speak in a way that the other person can understand and will make the person want to listen to you. This means trying your best to avoid talking for too long, or too abruptly or bluntly; to avoid inflammatory language or judgments of yourself or the other person; and to be concise and straightforward. Second, when you describe how you feel, use emotion words such as "hurt," "disappointment," "sadness," "irritation," "anger," and "annoyance." Try to use words that match the intensity of the situation (for example, in the preceding scenario, you might describe frustration rather than rage). If you can do so while being true to how you feel, try to use softer emotions (hurt, sadness, disappointment) more often than harder ones (anger, frustration, annoyance). People are more likely to empathize with you if you express softer emotions. You can also express your thoughts, but try to describe them objectively, without using judgments; for example, "I feel overwhelmed when I get home late and have to clean the kitchen."

Third, stay focused on what you want and don't get diverted (Linehan 1993b). In interpersonal interactions, it can be so easy to lose sight of your goal or your reason for starting the conversation in the first place. It's a lot like driving down a freeway toward your destination (your goals) but then inadvertently taking an exit to the middle of nowhere. For example, your partner might say, "Well, you never do the laundry! Why are you always on me about the dishes?" The skill here is not to be diverted and to return calmly to your request. For example, you might say, "I know what you're saying, but let's get back to those dishes on Thursdays. Then, maybe we can talk about the laundry."

Fourth, do what you can to use the interaction as an opportunity to enhance your relationship. Think of ways to ask for what you want that make the other person feel good about giving it to you. In the DBT interpersonal effectiveness skills, you do this by taking a kinder, softer approach and by expressing interest and understanding in what the other person has to say (ibid.). Think about how you might use humor or a lighter, gentler approach when you ask someone for something or refuse someone's request (ibid.). For example, you might say, "You're upset that I haven't done the laundry. I can totally understand that; I know you work hard, and it's frustrating when I don't help out. I feel the same way about those dishes."

Benefits of DBT Interpersonal Effectiveness Skills

Interpersonal effectiveness skills can help you to improve your interactions, manage and resolve conflict, and get your needs met in a way that empowers you and makes you feel more confident in your ability to deal with people. If, by learning some new skills, you find that you have better experiences with people, you might also improve your social support, feel better about your life, and develop more fulfilling and meaningful relationships. All of these benefits can help you to maintain whatever progress you have made in dealing with your anxiety-related problems. Here are some additional benefits of IE skills that are a little more specific to anxiety problems:

- Some people with anxiety disorders feel detached from other people. IE skills can help you connect with others and communicate your needs.

- Some people with anxiety disorders may not have much social support, so you can use IE to help establish new relationships.

- People with anxiety disorders may avoid conflict, which means that their needs are not met, and in the end, they feel worse about themselves. IE can help with this.

Exercise 4.6 Steps for Getting Your Needs Met in Interpersonal Interactions

Here is an exercise to get you started with some IE skills. First, think about something that you want someone to do for you. It might be that you want someone's help or support, or you might want someone to change a behavior (like washing the dishes more often). Choose a situation that is only mildly to moderately distressing or difficult. It's best to start with less-challenging situations when you are first learning new skills, just as you wouldn't choose to brave driving the streets of London if you had just moved to England (where people drive on the left side of the road, shift gears with the left hand, and navigate confusing roundabouts) after living and driving in the United States for many years.

1. Clarify your goals for each interaction. Ask yourself the following:

    What do I want out of this interaction? What are my goals for this interaction?

2. Develop a script for stating your needs and describing what you want. Make sure to complete all of the following sections.

    Explain the situation:

    Let the person know how you feel about the situation using "I feel" and "I think" statements:

    State your needs and what you want out of the situation. Be as specific as possible:

    Clarify up front how this will benefit the other person. Explain why giving you what you need or accepting your request will make things better for the other person:

Identify compromises you are willing to make. Make sure that you have thought about this ahead of time. Even if you don't have to offer a compromise, it is good to know how much you are willing to bend or give to reach an agreement. Write down the compromises you are willing to make here:

3. Practice this script until you feel comfortable with it. Practice as many times as you need. Try it out in front of a mirror, or with a close friend or loved one. Focus on your nonverbal behaviors (tone of voice, facial expressions) in addition to the words you are saying.

4. When you feel prepared (which does not mean you won't feel anxious), approach the other person and ask for what you want. Keep in mind that this skill (just like all of the others we have taught you) gets easier with practice. The more you practice asking for what you want in relationships, the more comfortable you will become, and the more likely you will be to get some of your needs met.

Try this exercise and see how it works, but remember one thing: try not to let yourself feel defeated or demoralized if you don't get what you want out of the situation. In the end, all you can do is your best, and even that will not always mean that things work out exactly as you would like. Even the most interpersonally effective people do not always get what they want. But even if the situation does not go as you would like, if you use these skills, you can take comfort in the fact that you did what you needed to do and were as skillful as possible. And, that can help a lot.

• William's Story

William lived with his wife in a very small town, where many people had known him personally since he was a young child. He worked as a carpenter (often doing jobs for local residents) and was involved in a very tight-knit religious community. After several bouts of depression, William began to discover that he probably had post-traumatic stress disorder related to past abuse by a family member when he was a child. During his periods of depression, he avoided leaving his home, did not attend church functions or activities, and failed to return calls about carpentry jobs. Over time, he became extremely ashamed and anxious, and he avoided people around town, because he was afraid of being judged, criticized, or pitied for his mental health problems.

Even when William's depression began to lift, he found himself still embarrassed and afraid to see people, and further, when he did see people, he had trouble making small talk and, in particular, being assertive. For example, he often said yes to huge jobs that he knew he didn't have time for. Then, he would do a less than optimal job or wouldn't finish the work and would wind up feeling even more anxious and ashamed. William had been so out of practice with social interactions that he needed to learn how to talk to people and also how to manage their demands, say no, and communicate his abilities realistically.

After learning DBT interpersonal effectiveness skills, he began to relearn some of the social skills he had lost, and he gradually started reemerging into the community by getting more involved in his church and reconnecting with others.

MOVING FORWARD

By now, we hope that you have a better understanding of what anxiety is and how it develops, what DBT is and how it might help you deal with anxiety, and the specific kinds of DBT skills we will teach you. Going through this workbook is much like building a new home. First, you need to lay the foundation, and that's what chapters 1 through 4 have been all about. Next, you need to put all the pieces of the home into place, and that's what the remaining chapters are all about. As we go forward in this workbook, you will learn ways to apply these DBT skills more specifically to the types of anxiety problems that you struggle with. By the end, we hope you will have a strong, safe bunker of skills to shelter you from your anxiety and keep you safe in the storm.

CHAPTER 5

Stress

Stress often goes hand in hand with anxiety and fear. In fact, these experiences go together so often that many people use the terms "stress" and "anxiety" interchangeably. What you may not know, however, is that even though stress and anxiety are closely related, they are not the same thing, and there are some important differences between these experiences of which you should be aware.

WHAT IS STRESS?

Just as we all experience anxiety, we all also experience stress. It is unavoidable. So what exactly is stress, and how is it different from anxiety? A much broader term than "anxiety," *stress* refers to the response your body has when you are facing circumstances that force you to act, change, or adjust to your environment. As you may remember from chapter 1, anxiety and fear serve very important functions. They are the body's way of telling us that we may be in a dangerous or threatening situation. Stress also serves a very important function. Basically, the experience of stress is an indication that your body's resources are being taxed or used up in some way.

You can think about it this way: Imagine your body as a giant computer. Now, computers are getting faster and faster every day, but in the end, even the largest and most complex computer has only a limited amount of processing power. So, if you run one small program on the computer, it will use up a little of your computer's processing capability. This means that the computer will have a little less processing power for other programs; however, with just one small program running, the computer's performance probably won't be affected that much. Now, let's imagine that you start running program after program on your computer. At some point, you will notice a decline in your computer's performance. Basically, the more programs you run on your computer, the slower the computer will be in managing each program. And, in extreme cases, if there are many programs running all at once for a long time, the computer could get so taxed that it crashes.

Our bodies work the same way. We have a limited amount of resources available to deal with the situations we encounter. Basically, we have only so much mental or physical energy available at any given time. The more situations or activities we encounter that use up these resources, the more stressed out, tense, or depleted we will feel and the less effective we will be in coping with these situations. In addition, the longer we stay in these situations or engage in these activities, the more our resources will continue to be depleted. As a result, we may have greater difficulties managing our emotions or feel more reactive, or our emotions may seem more out of control. Our concentration and attention may also suffer. We may have problems sleeping, and we may even increase our chances of becoming physically ill.

Now, one thing that people don't always realize is that stress can come from both pleasant and unpleasant situations. When many people think about stress, they think only about unpleasant or negative situations, ones that they don't like and would rather not have to experience, like losing a job, having money problems, or dealing with an illness, really unpleasant situations. In fact, even the word "stressful" has come to mean negative or unpleasant. However, pleasant events, situations that bring about positive emotions, can also lead to stress. For example, planning a wedding, having a baby, and getting a promotion can all be stressful. These situations may have benefits and you may be glad they happened, but they can also be a source of stress.

It is important to be aware of the types of events that bring on stress for you. The more aware you are of these situations, the better prepared you can be to cope with the stress when it arises. In exercise 5.1, we ask you to identify positive and negative current sources of stress for you.

Exercise 5.1 Identify Sources of Stress in Your Life

Close your eyes and take a few minutes to review the past several months of your life. Try to think back to a time when you felt very stressed out. What was going on at that time? Was it a positive event (for example, starting a new relationship) or a negative one (for instance, losing your job)? Write down all the positive and negative sources of stress that you have experienced recently. It may also be helpful to write down future sources of stress.

Negative Sources of Stress	Positive Sources of Stress
1. _____	1. _____
2. _____	2. _____
3. _____	3. _____

4. _____	4. _____
5. _____	5. _____
6. _____	6. _____
7. _____	7. _____
8. _____	8. _____
9. _____	9. _____
10. _____	10. _____
11. _____	11. _____
12. _____	12. _____
13. _____	13. _____
14. _____	14. _____
15. _____	15. _____

Now, before we talk about what you can do with stress, let's talk briefly about how stress applies to anxiety disorders.

STRESS IN ANXIETY DISORDERS

Although stress isn't usually considered a specific symptom of any one anxiety disorder, the one exception may be in the case of generalized anxiety disorder (GAD). To be diagnosed with GAD, a person must experience a variety of stress-related physical symptoms more days than not for the past six months, along with other symptoms, such as uncontrollable and excessive worry. Some of the stress-related symptoms of GAD include muscle tension, tiredness, difficulty sleeping, and concentration problems.

Although stress is not mentioned as a specific symptom of other anxiety disorders, stress certainly goes hand in hand with all anxiety disorders. A person with panic disorder may experience some of the physical symptoms of stress, such as muscle tension, during a panic attack or leading up to one. Someone with PTSD may experience high levels of stress as a result of constantly being on guard. In social anxiety disorder, a person may find social interactions very stressful. In general, anxiety disorder symptoms can be very difficult to cope with and can have a tremendous impact on a person's life. As a result, they often cause a great deal of stress. Basically, the experience of anxiety disorder symptoms in general can be incredibly stressful and taxing, taking away some of your resources to cope with other stressful life experiences.

MANAGING STRESS WITH DBT SKILLS

The good news is that several DBT skills can help you to reduce your vulnerability to stress, as well as to manage some of the consequences of stress.

Identifying Where You Experience Stress in Your Body

Before we go into these specific DBT skills, it's important to first identify where you experience stress and tension in your body. This is because physical or bodily experiences are often the first sign that you are under stress; they are the warning signals to which you need to pay attention.

Exercise 5.2 Where Do You Experience Stress in Your Body?

Try to think of times when you have experienced at least a moderate amount of stress in your life (around 5 to 6 on a scale from 0 to 10, where 0 means no stress and 10 means overwhelming stress). Now, try to remember where in your body you felt that stress. Listed below are some common places where people experience stress in their bodies. Put a mark next to the ones that are consistent with your experience. You can also add other places in your body that are not included in this list to the spaces at the end of the list.

_____	1. Shoulders
_____	2. Neck

_____	3. Jaw (for example, clenching or grinding teeth)
_____	4. Eyes and forehead (sometimes referred to as a tension headache)
_____	5. Lower back
_____	6. _____
_____	7. _____
_____	8. _____
_____	9. _____
_____	10. _____

Using Self-Care to Reduce Your Vulnerability to Stress

As mentioned previously, our ability to handle stress well has a lot to do with the mental and physical resources available to us. We can increase our available resources (and therefore reduce our vulnerability to stress) by making sure that you are taking good care of ourselves. In fact, this is so important that there is an entire set of DBT skills devoted to doing just that: taking care of our bodies so that we have more resources available for managing all of the demands and stressors in our lives (Linehan 1993b).

So, how can you make sure that you are taking care of yourself? Well, there are a number of things you can do.

MAINTAIN BALANCED EATING

One way to make sure you have as many resources as possible available to you to cope with stress is to feed your body nutritious food and maintain healthy eating habits (Linehan 1993b). Your body needs nutrients to live and function, so making sure you maintain a healthy diet will ensure that you have the needed fuel for your body. Think about it: your car doesn't perform well when it is running on fumes, does it? No, at that point, it can begin to malfunction or even stop running. Your body works the same way. You cannot function well if you do not have a full tank of gas, so make sure to give yourself the needed fuel throughout the day.

Now, healthy eating is actually made up of two parts. First, you need to eat regularly throughout the day, spacing out meals and snacks to "fuel up" several times throughout the day. Try your best to keep your blood glucose levels as stable as possible. Some research has shown that reductions in blood glucose can reduce your coping resources, making it harder to deal with stress and avoid harmful coping strategies (such as smoking, drinking, using drugs, and overeating) (Gailliot and Baumeister 2007). Keeping your fuel tank at a steady level will make you better able to keep driving and dealing with stress.

The second part involves eating foods that are healthy and good for you. You probably won't have as many resources available to manage stress if, every time you eat, you consume only junk food or processed sugars. So, make sure to get plenty of fruits, vegetables, whole grains, and proteins; these are the premium fuels to really help your body run at full capacity. There's nothing wrong with the occasional indulgence, but generally you want to eat a consistently healthy, balanced diet. If you are unsure about what to eat or how to maintain a well-balanced, healthy diet, you might consider talking with your family physician, meeting with a nutritionist, or consulting the Dietary Guidelines for Americans (www.choosemyplate.gov/guidelines /index.html) or Food and Nutrition information for Canadians (hc-sc.gc.ca/fn-an/index-eng.php).

MAINTAIN BALANCED SLEEP

In the same way that your body needs proper nutrients to run well, it also needs enough sleep (Linehan 1993b). Sleep is another source of fuel for your body, and without it your body does not run as well. When you don't get enough sleep, your physical resources are greatly depleted, diminishing your ability to manage stress. Basically, when you are sleeping, your body restores its resources and builds up the mental and physical energy for the day. So, if you don't get the full amount of sleep you need each night, your body won't have time to fully restore your resources, which means that you will have fewer resources available to you to start your day. And that means that you will have fewer resources available for managing stress.

Have you noticed that when you don't get enough sleep, you are more on edge, and things that normally wouldn't bother you seem to bother you a lot? That is probably because you don't have the same level of resources available to you for managing stress as you would normally have after a full night's sleep and, thus, aren't able to handle it as well. That is why getting a full night's sleep every night is so important. And, one way to make sure you get enough sleep is to maintain a regular sleep schedule, going to bed at about the same time each night and waking up at around the same time each morning. Regular sleep means more resources for managing stress.

This, of course, is easier said than done. People with anxiety disorders often have difficulty sleeping, experiencing periodic bouts of insomnia, difficulties falling asleep, or early awakenings fraught with worry. One way to deal with these problems is to use what's called *sleep hygiene*. Sleep hygiene involves a set of strategies you can use to improve your sleep (Pallesen et al. 2001). Usually, the first step is to improve your sleep area by getting rid of clutter in your bedroom and making sure it's an optimal environment for sleeping. Next, see if you can identify and change some of the factors that might make it hard for you to get a good night's sleep. Some of these factors might include taking long afternoon naps (short naps are okay), using caffeine, watching stimulating television shows, exercising, using alcohol or drugs too close to bedtime, and eating a large dinner. Do your best to change your behavior to optimize your sleep. Third, maximize your sleep efficiency. Sleep efficiency is the proportion of sleep to the amount of time spent in bed. So, if you spend eight hours in bed but sleep only six of those hours, your sleep efficiency is 75 percent. Basically, the idea is to get that number as close to 100 percent as possible by avoiding activities other than sleep (sexual activity is okay) in your bed. Don't work, check your e-mail, watch television, or have important discussions in bed. You want your brain to make a connection between bed and sleep, not between bed and being awake.

GET REGULAR EXERCISE

Another way to reduce your vulnerability to stress is to get regular exercise (Linehan 1993b). Regular exercise can actually make your body stronger, building up your physical resources over time. And this means that you will have more resources available for handling stress. Now, when we talk about getting regular exercise, we don't mean that you have to work out at a gym five days a week. Don't get us wrong: if you have the time and money to go to the gym that often, that is great and can definitely help build your strength; however, that isn't necessary to see the physical benefits of exercise. To get the physical benefits of exercise, all you need is to do some sort of moderate physical activity thirty minutes a day for five days a week. And this doesn't have to mean running or using exercise equipment. It could mean walking, gardening, vacuuming, walking up the stairs at your residence or workplace, or anything else that gets your heart rate up. The only thing that matters is that you do something moderately active for at least thirty minutes. And the more creative you are, the better. As mentioned before, one thing that can lead to stress is being busy and having a lot of demands on your time. This is the same thing that can make it difficult to keep a regular exercise program.

So, go easy on yourself and focus on getting exercise anywhere you can. If you have to go to the store, park as far away as possible so you can get in a bit of a walk. If you work in a multistory building or have appointments in such buildings, take the stairs rather than the elevator. If you need to clean your house, focus on making the cleaning as physical as possible, moving the vacuum rigorously and really throwing yourself into scrubbing the floors or polishing the furniture. Finally, riding your bike to work is another way to build exercise into your regular routine.

TAKE CARE OF ANY ILLNESSES YOU HAVE

It's also important to remember that physical illness can drain your body's resources, making it harder to deal with daily stressors. Therefore, one way to shore up your resources so that you can weather a storm or stressful situation is to take care of any illnesses you have (Linehan 1993b). So, if you think you are coming down with something or know that you have an illness, go to the doctor. Take appropriate medications. Make sure to get extra sleep. Get a lot of liquids. Have some chicken-noodle soup. Take a day off work or reduce your exercise routine temporarily. Basically, do everything you can to take care of that illness and restore your physical health. You'll be amazed at just how much better able you are to manage stress when you are physically healthy.

LIMIT ALCOHOL AND AVOID DRUGS

Another thing people don't always realize is that too much alcohol can take a toll on the body and use up a lot of the body's physical resources. In a similar way, taking alcohol or mood-altering drugs can tax your emotional resources. So, one way that you can reduce your vulnerability to stress and ensure that you keep your body functioning at the optimal level is to simply avoid using drugs and limit your alcohol intake (Linehan 1993b).

INCREASE YOUR SELF-EFFICACY BY DOING THINGS THAT MAKE YOU FEEL CAPABLE

Have you ever noticed that when you feel good about yourself, you handle stress better and don't seem to get as thrown by stressful situations as you do when you feel worse about your abilities or less capable? This is probably because stress can wear on you psychologically in addition to physically. So, feeling stronger and more capable psychologically translates into a heightened ability to handle and manage stress. Therefore, one simple way of reducing your vulnerability to stress is to do one thing each day that makes you feel capable and in control of your life (Linehan 1993b). It doesn't matter what it is; all that matters is that you are doing something that makes you feel capable.

Exercise 5.3 Begin to Reduce Vulnerability to Stress by Identifying Strengths and Weaknesses

Use this exercise to figure out what you are currently doing to take care of your body and the things you could change to help your body run at full capacity.

If you answer yes to some of these activities, congratulations! You are taking care of your body and reducing your vulnerability to stress in this way. That will help you have the resources to manage stress when it comes up. If you answer no, think about how you can begin to take better care of yourself. Begin by identifying three specific actions you can take to start to improve in this area.

Activity	Response (circle one)	Three specific actions you can take to improve in this area
Do you go to the doctor for regular checkups?	Yes No	1. 2. 3.
Do you go to the doctor when you notice you are sick?	Yes No	1. 2. 3.
Do you take your prescribed medications?	Yes No	1. 2. 3.
Do you eat several times throughout the day?	Yes No	1. 2. 3.

Do you eat fruits, vegetables, whole grains, and proteins?	Yes No	1. 2. 3.
Do you limit junk food and sweets?	Yes No	1. 2. 3.
Do you get at least seven to nine hours of sleep per night?	Yes No	1. 2. 3.
Do you have a regular sleeping schedule?	Yes No	1. 2. 3.
Do you try to do some sort of physical activity every day?	Yes No	1. 2. 3.
Do you exercise at least thirty minutes three days a week?	Yes No	1. 2. 3.
Do you limit your alcohol intake?	Yes No	1. 2. 3.
Do you refrain from using mood-altering drugs?	Yes No	1. 2. 3.
Do you do at least one thing a day that makes you feel capable and in control of your life?	Yes No	1. 2. 3.

Using Self-Soothing Strategies to Calm Your Mind and Body

A very similar set of skills to those described previously involves caring for your body and soothing yourself physically throughout the day. As with the skills for reducing your vulnerability to stress, you can use the self-soothing skills in DBT (Linehan 1993b) to prevent the negative effects of stress and increase your ability to manage the stress that you encounter. These skills can help you restore your resources throughout the day and continue to replenish those resources so that when stress arises unexpectedly, you can handle it better. The purpose of these skills is to care for and soothe your body by introducing comforting sensations to each of your five senses. Some of the sensations people find most soothing and comforting are described next (Linehan 1993b).

- **Touch:** Introduce sensations that soothe your body and feel good against your skin. Take a warm bubble bath. Sit in a hot tub or sauna. Get a massage. Play with your favorite pet, focusing on the feel of the pet's fur against your skin. Relax in the sun, focusing on the warmth on your skin. Hug a friend or loved one. Put on clothing that has a soft, soothing texture, like a warm sweater, a soft flannel shirt, a soft cotton sweatshirt, or a silk top. Wrap yourself up in a warm, fluffy blanket. Sit in front of a fire and focus on the warmth you feel.

- **Taste:** Sip a cup of hot tea or cocoa (or some other hot drink). On a hot day, drink something cold, or eat a Popsicle or an ice cream bar. Eat your favorite comfort food, such as macaroni and cheese, sushi, a grilled-cheese sandwich, mashed potatoes, fish and chips, or freshly baked bread. Eat dark chocolate (this also releases "feel-good" chemicals). Eat a piece of very fresh fruit.

- **Smell:** Go to a flower shop (and pretend you're shopping even if you're not). Burn incense or light a scented candle. Inhale the aroma of lavender or vanilla. Go outside and breathe in fresh air. Bake cookies or fresh bread, and breathe in the aroma. Smell fresh coffee beans, or brew some fresh coffee.

- **Sight:** Look at pictures of loved ones or a favorite vacation spot. Look at pictures that you find soothing or that relax you, like pictures of the beach, a sunset, or a beautiful mountain. Go to the beach and watch the waves hit the sand. Watch a sunset. Watch the clouds in the sky. Watch your pet or children play or sleep. Go to a playground and watch children play.

- **Hearing:** Listen to relaxing music. Listen to birds sing. Listen to children playing. Take a walk through the woods and listen to the sounds of nature. Sit outside at dusk and listen to the crickets. Go to the beach and listen to the sound of waves crashing on the shore.

Use the following worksheet to see if you can come up with some of your own self-soothing techniques. Anything you find comforting and nurturing might just do the trick!

Exercise 5.4 Identify Self-Soothing Strategies

See if you can come up with some self-soothing skills that would work for you. Focus on each of your five senses and different things that you find most comforting. See if you can identify five different activities for each sense.

Touch:
Taste:
Smell:
Sight:
Hearing:

Now that you have identified some self-soothing techniques that may work for you, see if you can use one or two of these techniques each day. If you do, you may very well find that you are better able to handle stress when it comes up.

Using Mindfulness Skills to Deal with Distraction and Poor Concentration

Stress can be very distracting. Often, when people are under a lot of stress, they find that they have a difficult time focusing on anything else. Is this one way in which stress affects you? When you are stressed, do you find it difficult to think about anything else? Do you find that you spend a lot of time thinking about the sources of your stress and the impact this stress has on you? If this is one way stress affects you, you may find that it gets in the way of accomplishing other things in your life, which can add to your stress by making you feel like you are behind in your tasks or not productive. Or it may take your attention away from positive things in your environment or aspects of your life that are not stressful.

Fortunately, DBT has a skill that can help you refocus your attention and manage this symptom of stress. Specifically, the DBT mindfulness skill of focusing attention on one thing at a time (Linehan 1993b) can be used to help you refocus your attention on whatever you are doing in the moment, making sure that you return your attention to the present moment and the task at hand when you are distracted by stress. As mentioned in chapter 3, this skill is all about doing one thing at a time: focusing all of your attention on only one thing and letting go of distractions. So, if you are writing, write. If you are playing with your children, play with your children. If you are doing something comforting or self-soothing, focus all of your attention on just that. So many times when people are stressed out, they believe that it will be better to try to multi-task and work on many things at once. They think that this will help them get more done and, as a result, feel less stressed. But, as common as that belief may be, it is just not true. Instead, focusing all of your attention on only one thing at a time and letting go of distractions that come up will help with your stress much more than multitasking.

So, the next time you find yourself getting distracted by everything that is causing you distress, take a deep breath and then bring your attention back to whatever you were doing in that moment. Focus all of your attention on just that one thing, throwing yourself into that activity and concentrating only on that. If you get distracted by your stress, notice that, and then return your mind to the activity at hand. Do this as many times as you need to, refocusing your attention again and again. Remember that minds get distracted; the goal of mindfulness is to simply notice when this happens and then to refocus your attention as needed, again and again.

This skill also can go a long way in helping you to endure stress in general. As Dr. Marsha Linehan recently told one of us, "When you just do one thing in the moment, you never really get overwhelmed" (personal communication). Have you ever noticed that what really stresses you out is not what you are doing right that moment, but a sense of doom or a bunch of worrisome thoughts about what you need to do in the future? Granted, sometimes the present moment, in and of itself, can be fairly stressful, but if you just focus on exactly what you are doing right now, rather than the mountain of things you need to get done at some point in the future, you will feel as if you are carrying around much less weight. When you are working on one task, stick to that task; when you walk from one place to another, just focus on the act of walking (rather than on getting to your destination or all of the things you will need to do when you get there). Practice this skill the next time you find yourself getting overwhelmed by all of the demands or stressors in your life, and see if it works.

Using DBT Skills to Deal with Emotional Reactivity and Stop Unwanted Behavior

Have you ever noticed that you are more likely to fly off the handle or easily break into tears when you are stressed out? This makes sense. When your resources are depleted as a result of excessive stress, you have fewer resources available to manage your emotions. Consequently, there may be times when you feel much more emotionally reactive or when your emotions feel out of control. When you are experiencing a tremendous amount of stress, it is hard to not be emotionally reactive. Although you may not be able to control how emotional you are, you can control your behavior. A couple of DBT skills focus on how to control your behaviors when you are experiencing intense emotions. Two of the skills that we believe can be most helpful in this regard are the mindfulness skill of noticing your experiences and the distress tolerance skill of focusing on the consequences of your behaviors before you act. Here is a list of steps you can take when you feel like you're at the end of your rope and almost ready to snap.

1. **Stop whatever you are doing.** Sit down in a comfortable, alert position someplace where you won't be bothered, and don't move a muscle.

2. **Step back and notice your experience.** Use the mindfulness skill of noticing your experience (Linehan 1993b) to step back in your mind and observe how you are feeling. Notice what emotion you are experiencing and where you feel it in your body. Use the spotlight of your attention to scan your body and figure out where you are holding tension, what your heart rate and body temperature feel like, and what other sensations you are having. If your mind wanders, that's okay; just return your attention to your body. Don't push any of your sensations away or try to escape them. Just notice them for now.

3. **Notice any urges to act.** If you feel really angry, irritated, or frustrated, maybe you have the urge to lash out at someone. If you feel despair, shame, or sadness, perhaps you want to rush away and curl up in your bed. Whatever you feel like doing, which we would call your *action urge* (what you feel like doing when you feel an emotion), just simply notice that. Notice what you feel like doing, observe and notice the urge or desire to act, and let it come and go, rise and fall like a wave on the ocean. Simply step back and pay attention to it for a little while. Don't push it away or try to keep it around. Try to visualize yourself riding this urge as if it were a wave on the ocean (this is the skill of "urge surfing," and it comes from Dr. Alan Marlatt's 2011 work on mindfulness-based relapse prevention) (Bowen, Chawla, and Marlatt 2011). See exercise 5.5 for practice in urge surfing.

4. **Think through the consequences of what you want to do.** One of the best ways to steer yourself onto a more effective course when you are stressed out and feel reactive is to think through what might happen if you were to simply act on impulse and do what you feel like doing. When you're stressed out, the immediate positive consequences of actions like yelling, drinking, using drugs, throwing things, and so on are likely to seem pretty attractive. So, you need to get your brain focused on the negative consequences of these behaviors. One of the ways to do this is to make a list of all of the consequences of various behaviors, both positive and negative, short term and long term. Exercise 5.6 can help you do just that.

The following exercise in urge surfing is adapted from our book *Freedom from Self-Harm: Overcoming Self-Injury with Skills from DBT and Other Treatments* (Gratz and Chapman 2009).

Exercise 5.5 Urge Surfing: A Mindfulness Skill to Cope with Urges

Find a quiet place where you will be relatively free of distractions and won't be bothered by anyone. Sit in a comfortable position. Write down how strong your urge is on a scale from 0 (no urge at all) to 10 (the strongest urge you have ever had). Then, write down how much you feel that you can handle your urge, using a scale from 0 (can't take it for one more second) to 10 (could handle it for ten hours straight if you had to). Imagine that you are standing on a surfboard on the ocean in a warm, tropical place. You can see the white, sandy shore in front of you, there is a slight breeze, and you can smell the salt of the ocean. There are a few fluffy, white clouds overhead, and the sun feels warm on your back. Really transport your mind to this scene.

Now, imagine that your action urge is the wave that you are about to catch. As your urge rises and becomes stronger, the wave gets higher, but you keep right on top of it. Imagine that you're an excellent surfer who can handle any wave that comes your way. As the urge gets stronger and stronger, the wave gets higher and higher until it crests. Imagine that you are riding the wave to shore. As you watch and surf the wave, notice what happens to it. Notice if it gets higher and stronger, or if it starts becoming lower and weaker. When it gets weaker, imagine that you are sliding into shore on your surfboard. When it starts to build again, imagine that you are back out there on the wave, just riding it. Keep doing this for about ten minutes, or until you feel that you have a handle on the urge and will not act on it. At the end, write down how strong your urge is on a scale from 0 to 10 and how much you feel that you can handle your urge on a scale from 0 to 10.

Use the following exercise to come up with as many short-term and long-term consequences of impulsive behaviors as you can. Make sure you fill in each of the four boxes in the table and include both positive and negative consequences. There are three important steps to remember about this skill: (1) write down only the important consequences; (2) memorize your list of consequences so that you can use it next time you need it without much thought or effort, or make a copy of this list and carry it with you; and (3) pay a lot of attention to the negative consequences of the problem behavior. Use this strategy to get yourself motivated to go down a different path when you're stressed out.

Exercise 5.6 Positive and Negative Consequences of Impulsive Behaviors

Use this table to help you focus on all of the consequences of impulsive behaviors, both positive and negative. First, identify your action urges, or what you feel like doing when you are at the end of your rope and feel as if you could snap.

Action Urge: _____

Then, fill in the likely consequences of doing what you feel like doing, making sure to focus on both the positive and negative consequences (both short and long term). Then, review the list and decide what will be the best choice for you, taking all of the consequences into account.

	Positive Consequences	Negative Consequences
Short-Term Consequences		
Long-term Consequences		

MOVING FORWARD

Stress affects us all. Many of us get irritated, a little stressed out, or a bit on edge many days. When you add anxiety problems on top of that, stress can be overwhelming. One of the most helpful ways to reduce stress is to shore up your resources by taking care of yourself on a regular basis. You can also learn to reduce the effects of stress by using self-soothing and other calming strategies. Finally, mindfulness, urge surfing, and focusing on the consequences of your behaviors before you act can help you stop yourself from making things worse by acting on your stress or aggravation. We hope that some of these DBT skills we have described in this chapter will help you get a handle on and reduce some of the stress in your life. In the next chapter, we discuss ways to manage worry and rumination.

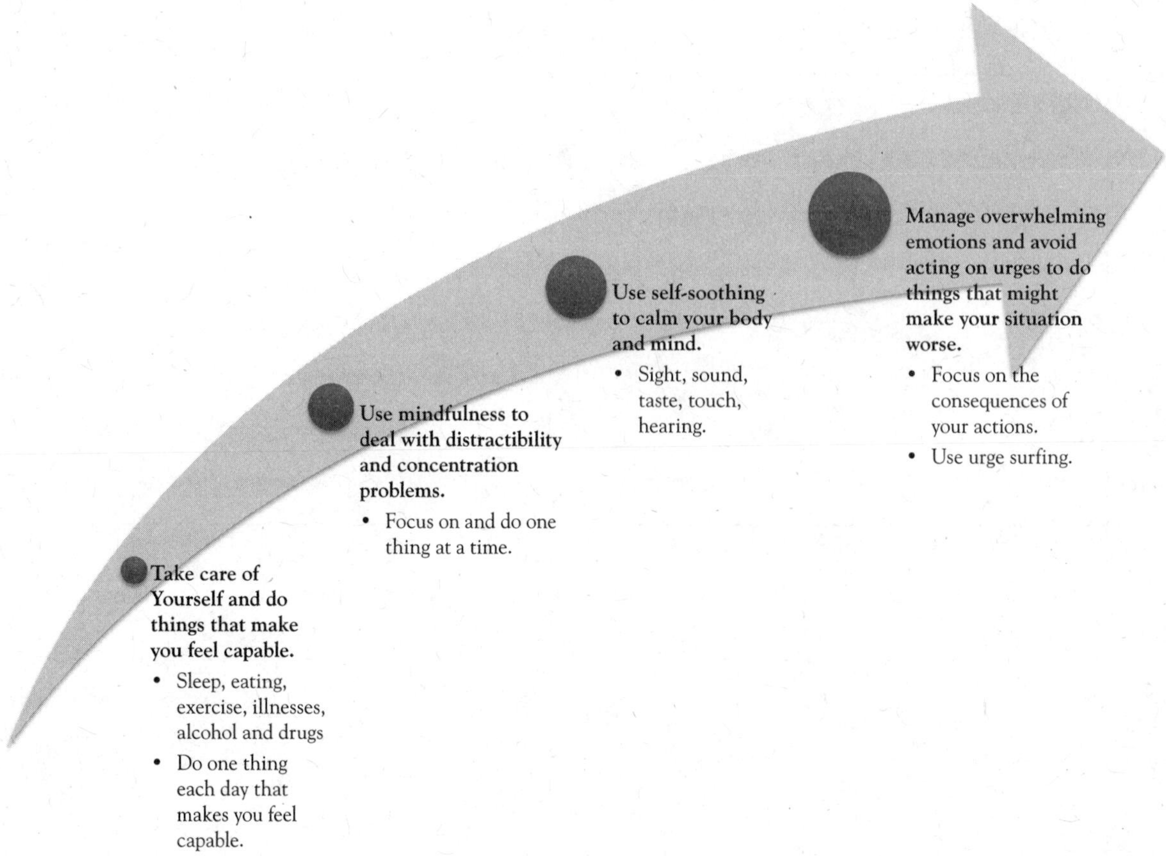

Manage overwhelming
emotions and avoid
acting on urges to do
things that might
make your situation
worse.

- Focus on the
  consequences of
  your actions.
- Use urge surfing.

Use self-soothing
to calm your body
and mind.

- Sight, sound,
  taste, touch,
  hearing.

Use mindfulness to
deal with distractibility
and concentration
problems.

- Focus on and do one
  thing at a time.

Take care of
Yourself and do
things that make
you feel capable.

- Sleep, eating,
  exercise, illnesses,
  alcohol and drugs
- Do one thing
  each day that
  makes you feel
  capable.

Figure 5.1   **Putting It All Together: How to Deal with Stress**

CHAPTER 6

Worry

Everyone reading this book (including the three of us who wrote this book) is probably very familiar with worry. Some people may worry more than others, and there may be times when you worry more or less. In the end, however, worry is a common experience for everyone (Tallis, Eysenck, and Mathews 1992). All human beings worry. There really is no way to get around it. From an early age, people are trained to focus a lot of their attention on the future, planning where they need to be, what they need to do, and so on. Combine this with the fact that life is often unpredictable and uncontrollable (and thus, stressful and anxiety provoking), and you have the perfect recipe for worry.

WHY WORRY?

As with all other behaviors that people engage in, worry serves a function. It does not occur randomly. It develops and then sticks around for a reason. Worry refers to future-focused negative thoughts about a number of different topics, such as your job, finances, family, or health (Roemer, Orsillo, and Barlow 2002). Another way to describe worry is "what if" thinking (Borkovec 1985). For example, when worrying, people may wonder, *What if I can't pay my bills next month?* or *What if my parents get sick?* When worrying, you are essentially identifying a problem that could occur in the future. Now, in some ways, this could be a useful process. If the worry motivates some kind of corrective action, prepares you for a definite upcoming negative event, or helps you come up with a solution to the problem, the worry served a very useful function. In fact, many people say that their worry is actually helpful for these reasons (Borkovec and Roemer 1995).

Before we begin to get into the ways in which worry can work against you, it is important to increase your awareness of what exactly you worry about. The following exercise provides a list of some common things that people worry about (Lindesay et al. 2006; Roemer, Molina, and Borkovec 1997). Check all that apply to you and add any of your own.

Exercise 6.1 What Do You Worry About?

	Mark all that apply.
	The quality of your intimate relationships
	Your intimate partner's level of commitment in your relationship
	Finding an intimate partner or starting an intimate relationship
	The quality of your relationships with friends or family
	The health or well-being of family members (such as parents or children) or friends
	Finances (such as being able to pay bills, save money, manage debt)
	Keeping up with household repairs
	Being able to find or keep a job
	Moving up in your job (for example, impressing your boss or getting a promotion)
	Getting good grades in school
	Managing schoolwork (for example, finding time to study and completing assignments on time)
	Graduating from school
	Your own mental health (such as managing stress, anxiety, or depression)
	Your own physical health
	Keeping up with day-to-day responsibilities (such as child care, housecleaning, and paying bills on time)
	Legal problems
	Political issues (for example, world or local events)

Do you have any other worries? List them.

1.
2.

3.	
4.	
5.	
6.	
7.	
8.	

Now, even though people may believe that their worry is helpful, more often than not, worry simply generates more anxiety. Here's how it works. What will happen to us in the future is unpredictable and largely out of our control. This naturally will bring up some anxiety. As a result, we may start to worry in an attempt to make things feel more predictable and within our control, bringing down our anxiety and all of its symptoms (such as increased heart rate) in the short run (Borkovec, Alcaine, and Behar 2004). However, when we worry, we are really only identifying a future problem that may or may not happen (and often a lot of them don't), which means that there may not be an easily identified solution. In addition, in the present moment, we really have no idea if the solution we came up with will work. So, basically, worry often takes the form of problem solving without the "solving" part. We are identifying a problem without really being able to come up with a definite solution (Borkovec 1985). As a result, our anxiety will then come back (and sometimes get even stronger), increasing the likelihood that we will worry some more.

Now, if you remember from chapter 1, many of the symptoms of anxiety are normal, everyday occurrences. This definitely applies to worry (Tallis, Eysenck, and Mathews 1992). As mentioned, everyone worries to some extent. However, for some people, worry can become so intense that it feels out of control and may constantly occur, greatly interfering with their ability to connect with and engage in positive and meaningful activities. When this happens, a person may develop GAD.

WORRY IN GAD AND OTHER ANXIETY DISORDERS

Generalized anxiety disorder is not uncommon. One survey of a large number of people across the United States found that around 4 percent of people had GAD at some point in their lifetimes (Grant et al. 2005). Constant and uncontrollable worry about a number of different events or activities is the central defining feature of GAD (APA 2000). In addition, in GAD a person experiences at least three symptoms of chronic anxiety (see exercise 6.2).

Exercise 6.2 Symptoms of Chronic Anxiety That Accompany Worry in GAD

	Mark all that apply to you.
	Restlessness or feeling on edge
	Becoming easily tired or out of energy
	Having a hard time concentrating, sometimes to the point where your mind may go blank
	Being irritable
	Having tension or pain in your muscles
	Having problems falling or staying asleep

In addition to excessive, uncontrollable worry and at least three of the symptoms listed previously, for you to be diagnosed with GAD, these symptoms also need to greatly interfere with some aspect of your life.

Now, just because you worry does not mean you have GAD. Worry does not have to be part of GAD to cause problems in your life. Worry can stand on its own. In addition, similar to other anxiety symptoms, such as panic attacks, worry is also seen in other anxiety disorders. For example, people with panic disorder may worry about the occurrence of future panic attacks. People with social anxiety disorder may worry about upcoming social situations and how they will perform in those situations. Someone with PTSD may worry about how to keep safe. Regardless, the function and consequences of worry are the same. Worry is an attempt to get away from anxiety or other unpleasant emotions, a strategy that works in the short term but tends to backfire in the long term. Indeed, most people who worry find that their distress or anxiety actually increases over time. In addition, when worrying becomes excessive, people often miss out on the pleasant aspects of their lives in the present moment.

FEATURES AND CONSEQUENCES OF WORRY

Worry can have a major impact on your life. Next, we review some common features of worry, as well as some of its negative consequences. We will also take you through some DBT skills that may be helpful in addressing each particular feature or consequence.

The Vicious Cycle of Worry: Getting Caught Up in Our Thoughts

Worry has a tendency to grab our attention. It can be really difficult to let go of worrisome thoughts. Think about it: worry makes us aware of problems we may encounter in the future. No matter how unlikely these future occurrences may be, they are definitely things we wouldn't want to have happen. Of course, we would want to attend to these thoughts and try to come up with a solution. As discussed earlier, however, the problem with worry is that often, there is not actually a solution. There also may not really be a problem. The anxiety that we experience may simply generate thoughts about potential problems in an attempt to establish some sense of predictability and control.

When people worry, they have a tendency to get caught up in their thoughts. In doing this, though, the worry cycle is maintained. Now, some people try to manage this by trying to suppress or push down their worrisome thoughts. Just like worry, this may be successful in the short run, but in the long run, those worrisome thoughts are going to return. In addition, they may come back even stronger or more intense. When we tell ourselves to not think about something, we actually increase the likelihood that we will think about it. By trying to not think about something, including worries, we naturally bring to mind the very thoughts we don't want to have. This is because you have to constantly be on guard that the thought isn't entering your mind, and by looking for it, you increase the chance that you will find it (Wegner, Erber, and Zanakos 1993).

So, as much as it may seem as if the simple solution to managing your worry and stopping the worry cycle is to try to not worry, we want to assure you that this will not work. Trying to get rid of worrisome thoughts will only make them stronger. Instead, DBT mindfulness skills (Linehan 1993b) provide a better (and more helpful) alternative for managing your worry and responding to these thoughts.

NOTICING THOUGHTS WITHOUT ATTACHING TO THEM

Rather than passing through our minds, coming in and then slipping back out, worry thoughts are "sticky." In fact, that's why we attach to them. It's kind of like we get stuck to them as they enter our minds and then have difficulty separating ourselves from them. Therefore, one of the most useful skills for dealing with worrisome thoughts is the DBT mindfulness skill of noticing thoughts without attaching to, reacting to, or acting on them (Linehan 1993b). In the *Skills Training Manual for Treating Borderline Personality Disorder* (ibid.), this specific skill is described as having a "Teflon mind." Basically, the idea is to allow thoughts to slide out of your mind in the same way that the nonstick Teflon coating on pans allows food to slide out of the pan when you are done cooking. Have you ever tried making an omelet or cooking a piece of fish in a pan that did not have a Teflon coating? The food tends to stick to the bottom of the pan and can be difficult to get out of the pan in one piece. In fact, that is one of the reasons why Teflon coating was invented: to make sure that food would not stick to pans. Well, the same rules apply to our minds. If we don't practice having a "Teflon mind," worrisome thoughts tend to stick to our minds rather than sliding out, as thoughts that are not distressing tend to do. So, the goal of this mindfulness skill is to allow your worrisome thoughts to pass in and out of your mind without getting stuck to them.

One way to do this is to picture placing each of the thoughts that goes through your mind onto a conveyor belt (ibid.). Conveyor belts tend to operate at a steady speed, moving objects slowly across a room. In the same way, you can picture all of your thoughts moving slowly and steadily across your mind. Don't try to change the speed of the conveyor belt, or to take thoughts off the conveyor belt. Just notice each thought passing through your mind, one after another. If you notice that the conveyor belt stalls, or the thoughts start piling up on one another on the belt, or the thoughts start falling off the belt, just notice that experience and gently return your attention to the conveyor belt, placing each thought on the belt and noticing as it moves through your mind. Practice this exercise for at least five minutes once a day.

LABELING THOUGHTS AS THOUGHTS

Another skill that can help you deal with worrisome thoughts is the DBT mindfulness skill of labeling your experience (Linehan 1993b). One of the reasons human beings tend to get so attached to and caught up in worrisome thoughts is that we "buy into" these thoughts as literally true. Rather than recognizing that these worries are simply thoughts our minds generated that may or may not be true or accurate, we believe our thoughts and take them to be the truth. Therefore, labeling a thought as just a thought is one way to keep yourself from buying into your thoughts or responding as if they were true. This skill will help you recognize that worries are simply thoughts generated by your mind, rather than a premonition of things to come. So, the next time you have a worrisome thought, make sure to label that worry as just a thought. For example, rather than thinking to yourself *My boss is upset with me* or *I'm going to fail this class*, make sure to describe these thoughts as just thoughts by consciously thinking something like *I'm having the thought that my boss is upset with me* or *I'm having the thought that I will fail this class*. Approaching your worries in this way and clearly labeling them as they are—just thoughts your mind has generated—will help you take a step back from your worries and not buy into them as if they were literally true. To help you with this, write down your worries on the following worksheet.

Exercise 6.3 Label Your Worry Thoughts as Just Thoughts

Use this worksheet to help you connect with the fact that your worrisome thoughts are just thoughts. Write down all of your worries here.

I am having the thought that _____

_____.

I am having the thought that _____

_____.

I am having the thought that _____

_____.

I am having the thought that _____

_____.

I am having the thought that _____

_____.

I am having the thought that _____

_____.

I am having the thought that _____

_____.

I am having the thought that _____

_____.

I am having the thought that _____

_____.

Not Being in the Present Moment

Another consequence of worry is that it takes us out of the present moment (Orsillo and Roemer 2011). As mentioned, worrisome thoughts are, by definition, focused on the future. Therefore, one downside of getting caught up in these thoughts is that you can miss out on your experience in the present. If you are constantly stuck in thoughts about the future, you may miss out on your life, which is lived in the present moment. And that means that you may miss out on some very pleasant and rewarding experiences. When people are not fully engaged in the present moment, they can feel as if they are not really living a meaningful and rewarding life. And, in some ways, this is true. If you're not fully present as you go about your day, you probably aren't living as rewarding of a life as you could if you were fully connected with what was going on around you. Being only partially present in your life will keep you from fully experiencing the meaningful parts of your life; you can begin to feel as if you are on automatic pilot.

NOTICING AND LABELING YOUR EXPERIENCE IN THE MOMENT

One way to combat this consequence of worry is to use the DBT skills of noticing and labeling your experience (Linehan 1993b) to help you get in touch with everything you are experiencing in the moment. Rather than getting caught up in your head and your own thoughts, focus your attention on noticing and describing whatever you are doing that moment. Ask yourself the following questions to help you fully connect with the present moment.

Exercise 6.4 Questions to Help You Connect with the Present Moment

Ask yourself these questions to help you get in touch with everything you are experiencing in the present moment.

Present external environment:

What do I see right now?

What objects do I observe?

Are there other people around? If so, what do they look like? What are they doing? What facial expressions do they have?

What do I feel against my skin?

What do I feel against my fingertips?

What am I hearing right now?

Are the sounds nearby or far away?

Present internal environment:

How do I feel right now?

What emotions am I having?

How does my body feel?

Am I cold, hot, or warm?

Are my muscles relaxed or tense?

THROWING YOURSELF INTO YOUR EXPERIENCES

Another skill that can help you get in touch with the present moment is the DBT mindfulness skill of throwing yourself completely into whatever you are doing in the moment (Linehan 1993b). The goal of this skill is to immerse yourself in your experiences, connecting with them completely. In addition to keeping you grounded in the present moment, this skill will also help you get the most out of what you are doing and fully connect with your life as you live. So, the next time you notice that you are getting caught up in your worries, practice bringing your full attention and awareness back to whatever you are doing at the time. Focus all of your attention on throwing yourself into the experience. If you get distracted by your worry, simply notice this, and then gently return your attention to the present moment and the activity at hand.

Emotional Avoidance

As mentioned earlier, worry may be effective in the moment at helping you distract yourself from your anxiety. People who struggle with worry also report that their worry helps distract them from more emotionally distressing aspects of their lives (Borkovec and Roemer 1995). Engaging in worry may make it seem like you are doing something to manage your emotions, but in the end it is really just a form of emotional avoidance. Worry really isn't doing anything to address your emotions (Roemer et al. 2005). Like all other forms of emotional avoidance, it ultimately will fail in the long term, resulting in those emotions coming back even stronger. Therefore, worry is actually counterproductive and may make your feelings seem confusing, unpredictable, and out of control.

Given that worry may be an attempt (albeit unsuccessful) to manage unpleasant emotions (Salters-Pedneault et al. 2006), one way of reducing your reliance on worry is by learning healthy and more effective emotion regulation skills, especially those that increase your acceptance of emotions. Here are some exercises that focus on ways of reducing emotional avoidance.

MINDFULLY NOTICE AND ATTEND TO YOUR EMOTIONS

If you find yourself often running from, avoiding, or escaping your emotions, then sometimes the best thing to do is the exact opposite: purposely look at your emotions, pay attention to them, notice them, accept them for what they are, and let them come and go. Worry can be a very unproductive way to deal with your emotions. Instead, if you mindfully notice them, you might find out that your anxiety, fear, or whatever other emotions you were avoiding are not quite as overwhelming as you thought. You might even learn that it's perfectly okay to have these emotions and that you really don't have to do anything to get rid of them.

Exercise 6.5 Practice Mindfully Noticing and Attending to Your Emotions

The next time you catch yourself worrying, you will likely find the following steps to be helpful. This skill involves paying close attention to the physical sensations of your emotion, or what you feel in your body when you feel a particular emotion. The idea here is to avoid getting entangled in your thoughts and to try your best not to escape or avoid your emotions; simply bring your attention to the physical sensations of whatever emotion you are experiencing. You'll find this type of exercise again in chapter 7, when we discuss how to deal with overwhelming emotions related to post-traumatic stress. This exercise, however, is much more focused on worry, so do it whenever you catch yourself worrying.

1. The first step is to catch yourself worrying. Identify that you are worrying and tell yourself, *Okay, I'm worrying again.* Describe the worrisome thoughts that are going through your mind here:

_____

_____

_____

_____

_____

_____

_____

_____

2. The second step is to turn your attention to your body and notice any sensations of emotion that you can identify. You might notice that your muscles are tense, your heart is beating hard or quickly, you have butterflies or a sinking feeling in your stomach, or you feel queasy or nauseated. Whatever you are feeling, simply pay attention to it and notice it. Keep your attention on your body. If your mind strays to other topics or you notice worrisome thoughts creeping into your mind, then gently guide your attention back to your body. Don't let yourself get involved with your worrisome thoughts. Just notice them and return your mind to your body again and again. Try to label or name your emotion, whether it's anxiety, dread, fear, trepidation, anger, irritation, shame, or sadness. Tell yourself that it's okay that you feel what you feel, that your emotion won't kill you, and try your best to simply let it be there for as long as it's there. See if you can watch or notice it with curiosity. See your emotion as an ocean wave cresting and then dissolving on the shore. Notice how transitory emotions can be; sometimes they're there one minute and gone the next. It's perfectly okay to have them; you don't need to get rid of or escape them.

3. Put words to your experience. Use the following space to describe what you noticed when you paid attention to the bodily sensations of your emotion:

_____

_____

_____

_____

_____

_____

_____

_____

MOVING FORWARD

As with all the skills we have discussed in this book, make sure you practice the previous skills regularly. Take your time. Worry can be very difficult to manage, because it feels as if it's working in the moment. The content of worrisome thoughts is also quite good at grabbing the attention. Therefore, being able to effectively use the skills we discussed in this chapter can take some time and practice. Although it may be difficult, increasing your connection with the present moment and turning off that autopilot can be an incredibly rewarding and meaningful experience. Finally, remember that the goal here is not to eliminate worry or never think about the future. That would be impossible and really not that useful. Instead, we would like you to commit to recognizing when you are getting caught up in your worry and redirecting your attention to the present moment, where you can then use some healthier emotion regulation skills to manage your anxiety or any other unpleasant emotion you may be experiencing.

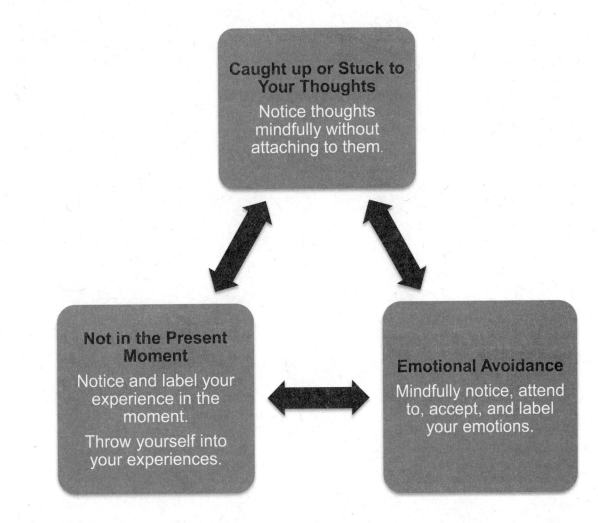

Figure 6.1   **Putting It All Together: DBT Skills to Manage Consequences of Worry**

CHAPTER 7

Flashbacks, Nightmares, and Other Traumatic Stress Symptoms

Studies have found that many people (more than half, in fact) will experience a traumatic event at some point in their lives (Kessler et al. 1995), and after the experience of a traumatic event, a person is at high risk of developing a variety of anxiety-related symptoms. The specific sets of symptoms that develop after a traumatic event are often referred to as *post-traumatic stress symptoms*. Post-traumatic stress symptoms can be quite debilitating, negatively affecting your relationships and ability to concentrate and stay focused, disturbing your sleep, and influencing the extent to which you find pleasure in activities that you used to enjoy. Later in this chapter, we will present some DBT skills that can help you manage some post-traumatic stress symptoms. Before we do so, however, we want to provide you with a quick overview of all the symptoms that can compose a post-traumatic stress response.

POST-TRAUMATIC STRESS SYMPTOMS

As the name implies, *post-traumatic stress symptoms* refers to a set of symptoms that develops after a traumatic event. Many different types of events could be considered traumatic, including being a victim or witness to physical or sexual assault, being exposed to combat, hearing of a loved one's unexpected death, being involved in a natural disaster, being in or witnessing a motor vehicle accident, or experiencing a life-threatening illness. Post-traumatic stress symptoms can be divided into three different groups: reexperiencing symptoms, avoidance and emotional numbing symptoms, and hyperarousal symptoms (APA 2000). Let's go over some of the specific symptoms that fall within each group.

Reexperiencing Symptoms

Reexperiencing symptoms are those that cause a person to relive or be constantly reminded of the traumatic event. There are five reexperiencing symptoms that a person can experience after a traumatic event:

- Frequent and intrusive thoughts or memories about the traumatic event

- Recurring nightmares about the traumatic event

- Acting or feeling as though the traumatic event were happening again (often called a *flashback*; we will go into this symptom in more detail later)

- The experience of distress after coming into contact with a reminder of the traumatic event (this may include a thought about the traumatic event or exposure to an object, person, place, or situation that triggers or brings up memories of the traumatic event)

- Experiencing bodily arousal (for example, increased heart rate) after coming into contact with a reminder of the traumatic event

Avoidance and Emotional Numbing Symptoms

As one might expect, the reexperiencing symptoms that someone can have after a traumatic event can be quite upsetting. Therefore, it is quite common for people to go to great lengths to try to prevent such symptoms from coming up, or in other words avoid them. These attempts make up the avoidance symptoms that a person can experience after a traumatic event. In addition, the fear, anxiety, and arousal that occur after a traumatic event can also diminish a person's ability to find pleasure in once enjoyable activities or experience a connection with other people. It is almost as if there were a block on a person's ability to experience positive emotions (whereas more unpleasant emotions are easily experienced). These are referred to as symptoms of *emotional numbing*. There are seven avoidance and emotional numbing symptoms that a person can experience after a traumatic event.

- Attempts to get away from or suppress thoughts or feelings that are associated with the traumatic event

- Attempts to avoid activities, places, or people that may be a reminder of a traumatic event

- Difficulty remembering important parts of the traumatic event

- Loss of interest in activities that were once found to be enjoyable

- Feeling disconnected or detached from loved ones

- Having a hard time experiencing the full range of emotions

- Feeling as though life will be cut short in some way

Hyperarousal Symptoms

After a traumatic event, a person may experience constant bodily arousal, which can have a number of negative consequences, such as difficulty sleeping, problems concentrating, or always feeling on guard and on edge. These consequences all fall under the larger category of *hyperarousal symptoms* that a person can experience after a traumatic event. There are five hyperarousal symptoms:

- Problems falling asleep or staying asleep

- Feeling overly irritable or having angry outbursts

- Having difficulty concentrating or staying focused

- Often feeling on guard or alert, as though there were some kind of danger or threat present (this symptom is referred to as *hypervigilance*)

- Feeling overly jumpy or being easily startled

IS IT POST-TRAUMATIC STRESS DISORDER?

After a traumatic event, only a percentage of people actually go on to develop enough of the previous symptoms to meet the criteria for post-traumatic stress disorder (PTSD) (Kessler et al. 1995). PTSD is diagnosed when a person meets a certain number of symptoms from each of the previous symptom categories at least thirty days after a traumatic event. The symptoms also have to negatively interfere with a person's life. However, even if a person isn't experiencing all of the symptoms required for a PTSD diagnosis, the person may still experience some negative consequences as a result of his or her symptoms. Therefore, regardless of whether you think you would meet the criteria for a PTSD diagnosis, if you are experiencing any of the symptoms previously listed as a result of a traumatic event, it is very important that you take steps to manage them in a healthy way. If you do so, you might avoid the development of PTSD and reduce the negative impact of post-traumatic stress symptoms on your life.

DBT SKILLS TO DEAL WITH POST-TRAUMATIC STRESS SYMPTOMS

Next, we discuss some of the features and consequences of post-traumatic stress symptoms, as well as ways that certain DBT skills may be helpful in coping with those symptoms and their consequences. As you read through the different symptoms that we discuss, keep in mind that not all may be represented. After a traumatic event, a number of anxiety-related symptoms can develop that aren't specific to a post-traumatic stress response. For example, after the experience of a traumatic event, some people develop panic attacks or worry. If you are experiencing anxiety-related symptoms as a result of a traumatic event that aren't listed here (for example, panic attacks or worry), look throughout the rest of this book. You will likely find those symptoms represented in other chapters, along with DBT skills for those symptoms.

Using Mindfulness and Distress Tolerance to Deal with Intrusive Experiences (Thoughts, Nightmares, and Flashbacks)

In this section, we will discuss intrusive experiences, which are very common among those who have experienced trauma. We call them *intrusive experiences* because each experience kind of intrudes into your brain without your inviting it. Such experiences include intrusive thoughts or memories, flashbacks, and nightmares.

Intrusive thoughts or memories about a traumatic event are very common, and the anxiety and fear that they bring up can greatly interfere with your everyday life. Different things that you might encounter throughout your daily life can easily trigger thoughts and memories of a traumatic event. For example, newspaper articles, television shows, sounds, smells, conversations, specific places, and people who are in some way connected to, or remind you of, a traumatic event can unexpectedly bring on a thought or memory about that traumatic event. As a result, these thoughts and memories can be unpredictable, and it often feels as if they appear "out of the blue." Not surprisingly then, these thoughts and memories can catch you off guard and be difficult to cope with. Intrusive thoughts and memories also can grab your attention, making it hard to focus on things you are doing. Further, the intense pain and distress they bring up can be distracting and overwhelming.

- ## Don's Story

Don came in and reported that he thought his mother might have sexually abused him when he was younger. His mother had recently died of cancer, and he had tremendous difficulty reconciling these memories of abuse with his sadness about his mother's death and his many positive memories of her. He also had experienced frequent emotional abuse by his father, who had often told him he was worthless and incompetent and would never amount to anything. Although he had worked through many of his difficulties in therapy, had improved his relationships with others, and was happy with his job, he frequently experienced intrusive thoughts and memories related to the possible sexual abuse and the things his father used to say to him. Brief images and memories would flash through his mind, he would feel guilty for even having these memories in the first place (as if it were marring the memory of his mother), and then he would experience a flood of thoughts similar to the things his father used to say to him (such as *You're an idiot! Why do you keep harping on that stuff? What's wrong with you?*). These experiences not only were incredibly painful and upsetting, but also made it very hard for him to focus on work or on any pleasurable activity in which he was engaged, such as movies or tennis with friends. As a result, he needed to learn new ways to manage and cope with these intrusive thoughts and memories.

Nightmares are another very common symptom that develops after a traumatic event. Nightmares can have a tremendously negative impact on your sleep and anxiety levels (Spoormaker and Montgomery 2008).

The exact cause of nightmares is unclear; however, some people think that difficulty with regulating emotions during the day may contribute to the experience of nightmares (Levin and Nielsen 2009). It could be that your brain is trying to process or deal with emotions you haven't been able to work through during the day. Therefore, by learning ways to better regulate your emotions and reduce vulnerability to distress, you may be able to reduce the frequency of your nightmares.

In contrast with nightmares, *flashbacks* occur when a person is awake and feels as though a traumatic event were happening again. Sometimes, a person might act out a traumatic event as if it were happening right then. As if it weren't bad enough to experience the trauma in the first place, your brain sometimes makes you live through it all over again. The severity of a flashback varies, ranging from being caught up in thoughts or memories (kind of like daydreaming) to being completely unaware of surroundings and losing track of time (sometimes referred to as *dissociation*). During a flashback, people sometimes hallucinate. Regardless of the severity of a flashback, it can be a very frightening experience. People with this problem may feel disconnected from the present moment and may also have difficulties bringing themselves out of a flashback if one is occurring, increasing their anxiety and fear.

Just as all these experiences (intrusive thoughts, flashbacks, and nightmares) have something in common (they're intrusive), the types of skills you can use to manage them are all pretty much the same. Mindfulness skills are perhaps the very first line of defense in dealing with intrusive experiences. In all of these experiences, your brain brings upsetting past experiences (intrusive thoughts and memories, flashbacks, or nightmares) or upsetting experiences generated in your imagination (nightmares) into the present moment. Therefore, one remedy for these symptoms is to yank your mind into the real, present moment. If you can focus your attention on the present moment, especially things that are outside of your body, it will be harder for the intrusive thoughts or memories to consume and overwhelm you. When you're experiencing a flashback, as real as it may seem, the events really are not happening right now. If you get your mind focused on what really is happening in the here and now, you might find that you are better able to ride out the flashback until it ends. With nightmares, you might wake up in a cold (or hot) sweat and find yourself doing things that you don't intend or want to do. In these cases as well, paying attention to exactly what is happening in the here and now can calm your mind, help to reduce the storm of upsetting emotions that follow the nightmare, and anchor you in the present moment. Similarly, with intrusive thoughts, if you get the spotlight of your attention out of your head and into what you are experiencing or doing in the present moment, you might take some of the power out of those thoughts. You might also notice that you are free to do whatever you want, despite them.

Now, when you practice mindfulness, you can focus either on internal experiences, such as bodily sensations, emotions, and thoughts, or on external experiences, like sights, sounds, and tactile sensations. When it comes to upsetting, intrusive experiences, we have found that the best way to start with mindfulness is to focus on external experiences. Sometimes the storm of internal bodily arousal, thoughts, images, and sensations is simply too much to manage in the moment when you are experiencing a nightmare or flashback. The best way to get grounded in the present is to pay attention to your external environment and external physical sensations.

The following exercise will take you through some step-by-step practice in observing, describing, and participating in the face of intrusive experiences. For each step, you start by just noticing your experiences and then move on to describing these experiences, and afterward we take you through ways to throw yourself into the present moment by immersing yourself in your activities. We hope that you find these to be helpful ways to manage distressing intrusive experiences.

Exercise 7.1 Notice and Describe Your Experiences, and Immerse Yourself in Your Activities

1. **Do a reality check.** Notice when you are either in the middle of a flashback or a bunch of intrusive thoughts or memories, or you have awakened from a nightmare (or even when you have awakened in the morning upset after a night of nightmares). Step back and observe, and clearly state the problem. Here is an example of the problem stated clearly:

   I have just been having a flashback or intrusive thoughts about . . .

   I have been having nightmares about . . .

   If you are in a flashback, remind yourself that whatever seems to be happening is not really happening. If you had a nightmare, tell yourself that the nightmare was just a nightmare and is not actually happening. If you are having intrusive thoughts, tell yourself *These are just thoughts; a thought is just a thought.* If you briefly write or describe to yourself exactly what is happening, this might serve as a reality check for you.

2. **Notice your experiences and describe how you feel.** Make sure that the lights are on in the room you're in. Start by sitting up in an alert position, with your feet on the ground. During this exercise, if your mind wanders, that's perfectly okay; that's what minds do. Just keep returning your attention again and again to whatever you're observing. That's the whole practice of mindfulness. Do this practice for about five to twenty minutes, or as long as it takes for you to feel a bit more grounded in the present moment.

   a. *Step back and pay attention, and then describe how you feel.* Bring your attention to the sensations of your feet on the ground or floor. Simply notice what the bottoms of your feet feel like. Notice any sensations of pressure, temperature, pain, tension, or relaxation. Notice what the surface of the insides of your shoes or the surface of the floor or ground feels like. Bring your mind to the feeling of your bottom on whatever you're sitting on. Simply notice any sensations of sitting. Remind yourself that you are here, right now, in the present, sitting in a room (or outside as the case may be), and that you are now free of the nightmare or that the flashback is just a flashback, not reality. Now, put your hands on your knees and notice the sensations in the palms of your hands. See if you can notice any other tactile sensations as well. Then, describe all of that—what you just noticed—using the following lines.

   _____

   _____

_____

_____

_____

_____

_____

_____

b.   *Notice and describe what you see around you.* If you are experiencing a flashback, do your best to observe and look through it at what you really see in your current surroundings. Gently ignore any visions of people, places, or events related to the flashback. Look at the floor and notice what you see there. Spend a minute or two just scanning the floor and noticing what you see there. Then, bring your eyes up to the walls and pay attention to what you see there. Notice the colors of the walls, any artwork on them, the lighting fixtures, the door frames, the doorknobs, and so on. Just step back mentally and notice these things. Also look at the ceiling, paying attention to the textures, colors, and objects you see up there. Finally, look at the chair, bed, or floor you are sitting on. Now, describe all that you just observed, using the following lines.

_____

_____

_____

_____

_____

_____

c.   *Step back, notice, and then describe what you hear.* Listen attentively to anything you hear inside the building, where you are sitting, or outside. Gently ignore any sounds that might be part of the flashback. In a really concrete way, just focus on exactly what you hear. For instance, you might notice the sounds of other people talking or walking around, the birds, the rain, the wind, or your own breathing. Just simply notice what you hear. Then, describe all that you just heard, using the following lines.

_____

_____

_____

_____

_____

_____

_____

_____

4. **Get active by throwing yourself into an activity right now.** The next step is to really throw your mind into an activity in the present moment. Remember when we talked about distress tolerance skills in chapter 3? Well, here you will use a combination of the distraction or self-soothing skills with immersing yourself in what you are doing right now. First, decide whether you need soothing or distraction. If your nervous system feels all wired up and you feel a lot of tension or bodily arousal, you might want to choose self-soothing. Alternatively, if you feel your mind edging back again and again to the flashback, nightmare, or intrusive thoughts, distraction might be your best choice. Ultimately, you can't go wrong with either, so you might want to try both. Here are some guidelines for how to throw yourself into your activities:

   - Do the activity with your entire mind, body, and soul.

   - Throw yourself completely into the activity so that you're completely immersed in it.

   - Do the activity with energy and vigor, and whenever your mind wanders, keep throwing yourself back in, almost as if you were jumping back into a swimming pool each time you found yourself crawling out.

   If you're using distraction, choose an activity that will pull your attention away from what is bothering you. So, choose something that is interesting or stimulating, something you can really get into, like the following:

   - Doing physical exercise (going for a run or a vigorous walk, or doing push-ups, sit-ups, aerobics, or yoga)

   - Doing puzzles, crosswords, or sudokus

   - Seeing, talking to, and interacting with other people

   - Shopping

   - Reading a very engaging book or magazine article

   - Getting out of your home and riding the bus somewhere

   - Doing arts, crafts, or hobbies

- Getting some work or studying done

- Eating (but not too much)

- Doing something that creates strong, distracting sensations, such as biting into a jalapeño pepper, eating spicy food, or showering with alternating cold and hot water

If you're using self-soothing, choose an activity that will be calming. When you are dealing with distressing events, such as nightmares or flashbacks, it makes a lot of sense to seek a little comfort or soothing afterward (or during). So, choose something that is comforting or soothing to you, something that calms your mind and your body. Here are some examples of soothing activities using your various senses:

- *Sound:* Listen to calming, soothing music, such as new age or classical music. One way to find such music is to look for the types of CDs people recommend for women who are in labor.

- *Sight:* Look at art, watch a calming nature show (nothing about hyenas attacking unsuspecting animals on a savanna), go someplace where you can see nature or beauty, look at photographs you find soothing, or look up photos or scenes on the Internet.

- *Smell:* Use aromatherapy candles or incense, smell flowers, take a bath with scented oils, smell fresh coffee beans, or make a cup of coffee or tea and just smell it.

- *Touch:* Wear a soft, soothing fabric; wrap yourself up in your favorite blanket; sit in a warm bath; take a calming, warm shower; run your fingers over something that has a nice, calming texture; get a massage or get your hair done; or do soothing physical activities with someone else.

- *Taste:* Eat comfort food; eat something with a calming, comforting taste or texture; or eat some candy or chocolate very slowly and mindfully.

- *Molly's Story*

Molly, eighteen, was referred to therapy by a community resource. She presented with severe PTSD relating to a sexual assault from her childhood. With a long history of abuse, she coped with her PTSD symptoms through drug use and sex work. She reported that sex work "brings [her] back" and makes her fear and shame associated with flashbacks "make sense." Molly's flashbacks were so severe that she sometimes believed the abuse was occurring in the present or had occurred in the recent past. During these times, Molly called her therapist or 911 in distress, because she felt that she was in crisis, saying "He [the abuser] is here!" This resulted in many police visits and threats to charge her with criminal mischief. Thus, it was essential that Molly practice mindfulness skills to bring herself back to the present moment. During these crisis calls, her therapist began to coach her in the mindfulness skill of nonjudgmentally labeling her experience, so that Molly practiced saying, "I am having a flashback in which I see an image of him." In addition, Molly placed a calendar on the wall and practiced observing the calendar to ground herself in the present year, which helped her to notice that she was not eight years old anymore, which was when the event actually occurred. Not only did this practice lead to a dramatic reduction in police calls, but Molly also found that the flashbacks were easier to tolerate.

Using Opposite Action to Reduce Avoidance

Given that post-traumatic stress symptoms are very distressing, resulting in high levels of anxiety and fear, and sometimes shame, guilt, and anger, it is not surprising that people experiencing these symptoms or emotions try to avoid them or avoid situations that bring up those symptoms. For example, a person may avoid large crowds, certain television shows, new people (such as going on dates), or new, unfamiliar places. This avoidance generally works in the short term, helping a person to avoid triggers of unpleasant memories, thoughts, and emotions associated with a traumatic event. However, in the long term, this avoidance often results in greater distress or increased separation from people or situations the person cares about. That is, a person may start to feel trapped or controlled by the post-traumatic stress symptoms and the avoidance behaviors that they bring on.

One antidote to avoidance is the DBT emotion regulation skill of *opposite action* (Linehan 1993b). As mentioned in chapter 4, opposite action basically involves doing the opposite of what you feel like doing when you feel a particular emotion. In the case of post-traumatic stress, often the emotion is fear. So, we will discuss next how to use opposite action to gain freedom from fear and avoidance.

Here's how opposite action works. Let's say that your traumatic event involved assault by a male acquaintance whom you met in a park in the middle of the day a few years ago. Over time, you have begun to fear parks and other places with concealing trees and bushes, and thus you avoid walking in such places. You might also have begun to avoid walking or traveling any distance outside alone, even during the day (after all, you were assaulted in the middle of the day), and perhaps you even generally avoid men. You eventually find that your life has become narrower, because there are so many people and places that you avoid.

Well, opposite action works by helping your brain to figure out which of these places or people are not actually dangerous and don't need to be avoided. Once your brain makes that connection, your fear tends to diminish, you stop wanting to avoid things or people, and your life opens up so that you have more freedom to go where you want to go and do what you want to do. In this way, opposite action is a lot like exposure therapy (Linehan 1993b), which we described in chapter 2 and with which you might have had some experience yourself.

Opposite action, in this case, would involve actively doing the opposite of what your fear tells you to do. Let's say your fear tells you to avoid riding the bus in the middle of the day because someone might assault you on the bus. Well, opposite action would involve actively riding the bus in the middle of the day as much as possible so that your brain learns that it's safe to ride the bus. Let's say you're afraid of walking in a public park at noon. Opposite action would involve repeatedly walking on purpose in a public park at noon, until your fear diminishes.

Now, you might be thinking *Hey, that's not safe! What if I actually get harmed or assaulted?* Well, here's an important point to remember about opposite action: You should only take opposite action for fear in situations where your fear *probably won't come true.* So, you wouldn't, for example, choose to walk in the dark through a dangerous neighborhood. If you're afraid of walking through that neighborhood, you probably have good reason to be afraid, and avoidance is a good idea. On the other hand, you can never be 100 percent sure that a situation will be safe. So, when you get started with your bus riding or walking through a park, you might want to make sure that you are much more likely to be safe than unsafe.

For instance, one of us worked with a woman who was in this exact situation: She had been assaulted by a male acquaintance whom she met in a park at midday. But she loved nature and running, and she didn't want to avoid parks in the daytime for the rest of her life. So her version of opposite action was to repeatedly visit the park but ensure that she did so safely, such as by avoiding listening to music while running and sticking to well-used trails.

Please see exercises 7.2 to 7.5 for the steps involved in using opposite action.

Exercise 7.2 Opposite Action Step 1: Figure Out What You Are Avoiding

In this first set of steps, you identify people, places, and situations that make you afraid and that you avoid. These steps will help you figure out what you're avoiding and many of the places in your life where you can use opposite action. Under "Situation," describe briefly a few key situations that you tend to be afraid of and avoid. Under "Fear," rate your fear of these situations on a scale from 0 (not at all afraid!) to 10 (maximum fear possible). Then, under "Avoidance Behaviors," briefly describe what you do to avoid these situations or escape from them. The following example will get you started. Let's say that you generally avoid places or situations where you perceive danger, such as public parks, buses, or places where you might end up alone with men.

Situation	Fear	Avoidance Behaviors
Walking through park in the afternoon	8	*Avoid parks day and night; walk on other side of street from parks; decline invitations from others to go to the park*

Exercise 7.3 Opposite Action Step 2: Figure Out Your Emotions and Action Urges

This next set of steps helps you determine how and when to use opposite action in the moment when you are afraid or want to avoid situations and people.

Determine your emotion and your action urge. Your emotion is the emotional state that you are in, and in this case we're talking about fear-related emotions, such as anxiety, fear, nervousness, and trepidation. Your action urge is what you feel like doing when you have this emotion. Remember the example from exercise 7.2, in which you tend to generally avoid situations where you are around men or alone with men? Well, if you are in a coffee shop and suddenly realize that you and one man are the only customers there, your emotion might be fear (let's say 7 on the 0-to-10 scale). Your action urge, or what you feel like doing, might be to pack up and leave, and perhaps you feel that urge at a level of 8 out of 10.

Emotion	Intensity	Action Urges	Intensity
Fear, nervousness	*7*	*Pack up, leave, watch the man's every move, hide in the back of the coffee shop*	*8*

Exercise 7.4 Opposite Action Step 3: Determine Whether Your Fear Is Justified

If your fear is *justified*, that means that what you're afraid of (in this example, let's say you're afraid you'll be attacked) might very likely occur. If your fear is *unjustified*, that means that what you are afraid of is very unlikely to occur. So, if you think of it in terms of a fire alarm, a true alarm (when there really is smoke and a fire) is like a justified fear. A false alarm (when the alarm goes off, but there's no fire or smoke) is like an unjustified fear.

Use opposite action for fear only if your fear is unjustified. For example, if the man in the coffee shop really was going to attack you, then it would be best to do exactly what you feel like doing and leave, rather than to do the opposite of what you feel like doing, which would be to stick around. Generally, fear is justified when there is an imminent threat to your life, safety, or well-being. Use the columns below to figure out whether your fear is justified. Really think it through, and ask yourself *Is there really reason to believe that my life, safety, or well-being is threatened in this situation?* If you answer no to all three, then your fear is unjustified, and it's a good idea to use opposite action. Let's say that your feared event is that the man will corner you and attack you. Think about, instead, the most likely event. Think of whether this poses any threat to your life, safety, or well-being.

Most Likely Event	Threat to Life	Threat to Safety	Threat to Well-being
That man will leave me alone.	*No*	*No*	*No*

Exercise 7.5 Opposite Action Step 4: Figure Out and Do the Opposite Action

The final steps are to figure out and then actually do the opposite actions. The opposite actions are the actions that are completely opposite to your action urges, or what you feel like doing. So, here, you revisit your action urges and then write down in the other column what the opposite action would be. This can be a little tricky, so we have included some examples for you. It is important to remember that you are to take the action that is opposite to what you feel like doing, or your action urge. It is also important to keep taking this action over and over again until your brain learns that the situation is safe rather than dangerous. Under the "Helpful" column, rate from 0 (not at all helpful, no reduction in fear) to 10 (extremely helpful, fear went way down) how helpful the opposite action was in reducing your fear. Remember, however, that opposite action often works over the long term rather than immediately in the short term.

We might suggest that you choose some of the situations you identified in exercise 7.2 and then gradually work through each of them, using these worksheets and taking opposite action where indicated.

Action Urges	Opposite Actions	Helpful?
Pack up and leave.	*Stay in the coffee shop, continue to read my book, sit confidently, and act like things are safe.*	6/10
Watch the man's every move.	*Ignore the man (unless he actually does something concerning), focus on my book and my food or coffee, don't be hypervigilant or constantly on the lookout for danger.*	7/10

Using Mindfulness to Deal with Overwhelming Emotions and Problems Managing Emotions

Going through a traumatic event can have a huge impact on how you experience and manage your emotions. After a traumatic event, your emotions may feel much more intense or out of control. They may change suddenly or without warning. In addition, as discussed previously, sometimes after a traumatic event, people have difficulty connecting with positive emotional experiences. This is called "emotional numbing." However, negative emotions (for example, anger, sadness, and fear) may be experienced very strongly. A person may feel consumed by these emotions. As a result, emotions may be more difficult to manage.

When the volume is turned up on an emotion, it can be harder to sit with, tolerate, and manage that emotion. It may also be harder to control your behavior when emotions are very intense. Very intense emotions make you more likely to want to just get away from those emotions as quickly as possible, leading you to be more likely to engage in impulsive or risky behaviors. An *impulsive behavior* is any action that is done quickly and rashly, and with little thought about the potential consequences of engaging in that behavior. Such behaviors include substance use, deliberate self-harm (for example, cutting or burning yourself), and binge eating. Although these behaviors work well in the short term at quickly reducing the intensity of an unpleasant emotion, they are associated with a number of long-term negative consequences. Also, because they don't really deal with the emotion (they just push it down or suppress it or distract you temporarily), the emotion that you were trying to get away from will come back, often stronger than before.

Fortunately, there are a number of DBT skills designed for tolerating and managing intense emotional experiences. These skills may be particularly helpful for someone who has experienced a traumatic event and is having difficulty managing or sitting with intense, unpleasant emotions.

One very effective way to cope when you're having difficulty sitting with intense, unpleasant emotions is mindfulness. One mindfulness skill in particular can be especially helpful here. Dr. Marsha Linehan (1993b) calls this skill *mindfulness of current emotion*, and it involves simply stepping back, observing, and paying attention to the physical sensations of your current emotional state. We're sure that this doesn't sound like loads of fun when you're struggling with intense, unwanted emotions, but paradoxically, by allowing yourself to enter into, watch, and experience your emotions, you might find that you are more likely to achieve freedom from them.

Sometimes, the only way to escape misery is to stop trying to escape misery and instead enter into and pay attention to it. Mindfully noticing and paying attention to your emotions can help you learn to better tolerate the unpleasant aspects of your emotions, so that the next time they arise, they feel more manageable and tolerable. The more you do this, the more you will notice that emotions don't last forever; they usually wax and wane without your having to do anything to change or get rid of them. Also, if you get a lot of practice just sitting with and attending to your emotions and your urges to escape them, you might improve your ability to stop yourself from using impulsive behaviors to escape or avoid emotions (such as drinking, using drugs, self-harming, having outbursts, and engaging in reckless behaviors).

Exercise 7.6 Pay Attention to and Notice Your Emotional State

The next time you have time and feel a moderately strong emotion (let's say at least 6 on a scale where 0 means no emotion and 10 means the most intense emotion possible), find a quiet place to sit in an alert, upright position, with your feet flat on the ground.

1. Start by bringing your attention to your body, and notice where in your body you feel the emotion (Linehan 1993b). Scan your body from head to toe, paying attention to the sensations in each part of your body as you go. Spend about ten seconds on each area of your body, just stepping back in your mind, paying attention, and noticing your sensations. This exercise is similar to the body scan technique developed by Dr. Jon Kabat-Zinn, an expert on mindfulness-based treatment (Kabat-Zinn 1990).

2. Once you have used your attention to scan your body, zero in on those parts of your body where you feel the emotion. For instance, you might feel tension in your shoulders and neck, an adrenaline rush in your chest, or a pounding or racing sensation in your heart. Zero in and focus on those areas where you feel the sensations of your emotion. Watch the sensations rise and fall as you would watch a wave on the ocean.

3. Keep focusing on the physical sensations of your emotion without escaping or avoiding them. Don't allow yourself to try to get rid of the emotion, push it away, avoid it, or escape it, or to distract your mind with activities or thoughts. No avoidance allowed here. Simply watch these physical sensations as if they were waves on the ocean, noticing how they change, increase, or decrease. Do this for about five to ten minutes, or until the emotion subsides or you have to go do something else.

Dealing with Relationship Problems

After a traumatic event, many people develop problems with interpersonal relationships (Beck et al. 2009). They may feel disconnected from others. After a traumatic event, shame and guilt are common emotional experiences that can definitely interfere with interpersonal relationships, making it difficult to be intimate with or close to people you love and care for (Dorahy 2010).

Anger and irritability, common post-traumatic stress symptoms (Novaco and Chemtob 1998), can also interfere with relationships. After a traumatic event, a person may have more difficulty controlling anger or aggressive behavior, potentially causing loved ones to keep their distance or feel as if they were "always walking on eggshells." Alternatively, after a traumatic event, some people try to avoid all conflict. They may avoid expressing their needs or desires in a relationship for fear of upsetting another person or causing a potential argument. They may fear that their post-traumatic stress symptoms will cause loved ones to leave them. However, if you don't express your needs, you may cultivate resentment, or you may miss out on opportunities to receive needed social support, a very important factor in recovering from a traumatic event (Agaibi and Wilson 2005).

Use exercise 7.7 to prioritize and communicate your needs if you are having difficulty doing so. We have included an example for you. As you can see, there are a few steps, the first of which is to identify your needs and goals. The next step is to figure out how you would state them to the person in question. The third step is to practice a few times, alone or with someone else. And, of course, the final step is to actually try it out and see how it goes. If you really learn these skills, you might find that you actually prevent the types of conflict that happen when you bottle up your needs over a prolonged period, or when you express them in an angry or frustrated manner.

Exercise 7.7 Steps for Getting Your Needs Met in Interpersonal Interactions

1. Describe the problem (to yourself, so that you're really clear on what's wrong).

    When I get anxious and panicky before we go out, my boyfriend gets angry with me and says I have mental health problems and am making it hard for us to get out and see people or have any fun.

2. Clarify your goals for the interactions. Ask yourself the following questions:

    What do I want out of this interaction? What are my goals for this interaction?

    I want my boyfriend to stop getting so angry and criticizing me when I have a hard time leaving the house. I also want him to feel good about me and the relationship, and I want our discussion to bring us closer. I want to feel like I have a right to my feelings and that my needs are important.

3. Develop a script for stating your needs and describing what you want. Make sure to complete all of the following sections. Wherever possible, own your feelings and thoughts by using "I" statements, avoid being judgmental or accusatory, avoid inflammatory language (like "always" and "never") and name-calling, and, when you have an option, try to express "softer" (hurt, sadness, fear) rather than harder (anger, irritation, frustration) emotions.

    Explain the situation:

    I have noticed that you often seem upset and tell me how frustrating it is for you when I am afraid to go out.

    Let the person know how you feel about the situation using "I feel" and "I think" statements:

    Although I know it must be really frustrating for you, I feel hurt and sad when you tell me that there's something wrong with me for being so afraid.

    State your needs and what you want out of the situation. Be as specific as possible:

    I would like it if you could try to have a less frustrated edge in your voice and spend a little time listening to me when I tell you how afraid I feel.

Clarify up front how this will benefit the other person. Explain why giving you what you need or accepting your request will make things better for the other person:

If you do this, I would feel a lot less hurt and a lot closer to you, and I'd be willing to try harder to go outside my comfort zone.

Identify compromises you are willing to make. Make sure that you have thought about this ahead of time. Even if you don't have to offer a compromise, it is good to know how much you are willing to bend or give to reach an agreement. Write down the compromises you are willing to make here:

I will do my best, when I can, to push myself to get out when it's really important to you and to get some help for this problem, as I know it's affecting our relationship.

4. Practice this script until you feel comfortable with it. Practice as many times as you need to. Try it in front of a mirror, or with a close friend or loved one. Focus on your nonverbal behaviors (tone of voice, facial expressions) in addition to the words you are saying.

When you feel prepared (which does not mean you won't feel anxious), approach the other person and ask for what you want. Keep in mind that this skill (just like all of the others we have taught you) gets easier with practice. The more you practice asking for what you want in relationships, the more comfortable you will become and the more likely you are to get some of your needs met! You may also want to pair this skill with some of the skills for tolerating anxiety, including deep breathing (exercise 2.1) and PMR (exercise 10.4).

MOVING FORWARD

Post-traumatic stress symptoms can be very challenging to manage on a day-to-day basis, and it is important for you to have some tools for dealing with these experiences and minimizing their negative impact on your life. Several DBT skills, such as mindfulness and distress tolerance skills for getting grounded and dealing with flashbacks and nightmares, opposite action for combating avoidance, mindfulness of your emotions for helping you regulate and tolerate emotions, and interpersonal effectiveness skills for identifying and communicating your needs, can help. We hope that you find our suggestions and exercises to be practical and helpful. We would also recommend that you consider other skills discussed in chapters 3 and 4, and the rest of the book, and how you might also use them to deal with problems related to post-traumatic stress. In the next chapter, we go over symptoms of panic attacks and panic disorder, and discuss how to use DBT to manage them effectively.

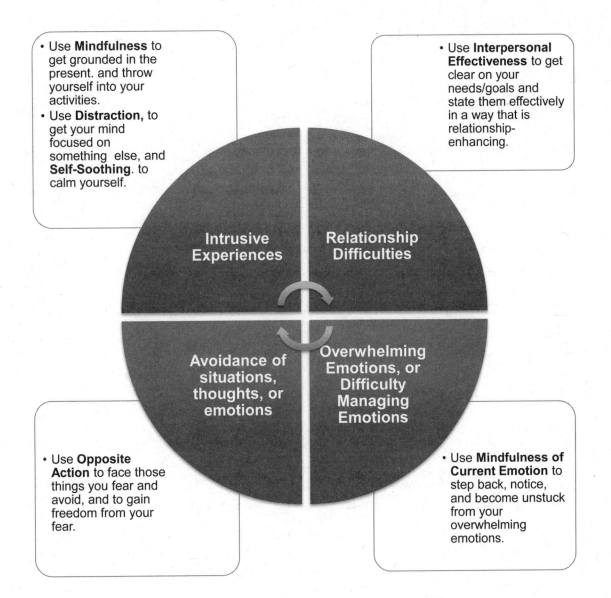

- Use **Mindfulness** to get grounded in the present. and throw yourself into your activities.
- Use **Distraction,** to get your mind focused on something else, and **Self-Soothing**. to calm yourself.

- Use **Interpersonal Effectiveness** to get clear on your needs/goals and state them effectively in a way that is relationship-enhancing.

Intrusive Experiences

Relationship Difficulties

Avoidance of situations, thoughts, or emotions

Overwhelming Emotions, or Difficulty Managing Emotions

- Use **Opposite Action** to face those things you fear and avoid, and to gain freedom from your fear.

- Use **Mindfulness of Current Emotion** to step back, notice, and become unstuck from your overwhelming emotions.

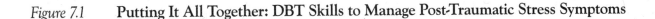

Figure 7.1   **Putting It All Together: DBT Skills to Manage Post-Traumatic Stress Symptoms**

CHAPTER 8

Panic Attacks

Panic attacks, or the sudden experience of intense fear or terror, can be found to occur in most anxiety disorders and are the main symptom of panic disorder in particular. However, as you may remember from the first chapter, panic attacks are actually a very common experience, even for people who haven't been diagnosed with an anxiety disorder. Panic attacks can also be very frightening and may have a major impact on a person's life. Fortunately, DBT skills can be incredibly useful in reducing the impact of a panic attack and in potentially eliminating panic attacks altogether. Now, before we go into the specific DBT skills that can be helpful for panic attacks, it is important to go over what panic attacks are, where they come from, and what kind of impact they can have on a person's life.

WHAT ARE PANIC ATTACKS?

If you have ever experienced a panic attack, chances are that you are probably well aware of what a panic attack is and what it feels like. There really is no mistaking a panic attack. A panic attack is much more than just strong anxiety or fear. Panic attacks are basically your body's fight-or-flight system going off unexpectedly. It is a "false alarm" (Bouton, Mineka, and Barlow 2001). During a panic attack, your body is essentially telling you that you are in some kind of immediate danger, even if a threat really isn't present. We'll talk more a little later in this chapter about why this may happen. Someone who experiences a panic attack has very strong feelings of fear, terror, or discomfort that arise quickly and intensely (APA 2000). A panic attack can be expected or unexpected. Panic attacks that are unexpected or occur without warning are also sometimes described as "out of the blue," spontaneous, or uncued. Many of the first panic attacks that people ever experience occur without warning.

Left alone, a panic attack will be relatively short lived, lasting just a few minutes (even though it may *feel* as if it lasts longer). However, how you respond to a panic attack can determine whether the panic attack persists for a longer period of time. You see, when a panic attack occurs, unfortunately there isn't too much that you can do about it except to let it run its course. You essentially have to wait for that false alarm to turn off. Now, if you try to avoid the symptoms of a panic attack or push them away, that alarm can persist or sometimes even get stronger.

Don't get us wrong; it makes sense that someone would want to try to get away from a panic attack as quickly as possible, as it is a really scary and unpleasant experience. In the end, though, trying to fight or escape a panic attack just fuels it and makes it stronger. Therefore, as scary as a panic attack can be, the best bet is to simply ride it out until it passes. Later we will walk you through some DBT skills that may make it easier to sit with the discomfort of a panic attack.

During a panic attack, people may feel a variety of sensations in their bodies, including increased heart rate, sweating, shortness of breath, and dizziness. In addition, people often have certain fearful thoughts during a panic attack, such as *I'm going crazy* or *I'm going to die*. In fact, because the physical sensations and fear that accompany a panic attack are so intense, it is very common for people who experience panic attacks to think that they are having a heart attack, prompting a visit to the emergency room, a place where many people with panic attacks first try to get help (Swinson et al. 1992).

Listed next are some common sensations that people experience when they are having a panic attack. The most common symptoms are increased heart rate, dizziness, trembling, and fear of losing control (Barlow 2002c). To qualify as a panic attack, at least four of the symptoms described next must be experienced. If you have fewer than four of these symptoms, you may be experiencing what is called a *limited-symptom panic attack*. Limited-symptom panic attacks are less common than standard panic attacks and generally less intense. However, they may still have some of the same negative consequences that accompany full-symptom panic attacks (ibid.; Rapee, Craske, and Barlow 1990). Regardless of whether you tend to experience full-symptom or limited-symptom panic attacks, it is important for you to be aware of the symptoms you generally experience when you have a panic attack. This information will allow you to tailor to these particular symptoms the DBT skills we describe next.

Exercise 8.1 Identify Your Panic Attack Symptoms

Mark all that apply.

	Racing heart or feeling your heart pounding
	Sweating
	Shaking
	Shortness of breath or difficulty catching your breath
	Feeling as though you were choking
	Pains or discomfort in your chest
	Feeling sick to your stomach

	Dizziness, faintness, light-headedness
	Feeling as though things around you were unreal, almost as if you were in a dream
	Feeling separated or detached from yourself (kind of as if you were watching yourself from afar)
	Fears or thoughts that you will lose control
	Fears or thoughts that you are going crazy
	Fearing that you are about to die
	Numbness or tingling in your extremities
	Chills or hot flashes

Do you have any other symptoms? List them.

Now that you know what symptoms you experience when you have a panic attack, let's go over some more information on panic attacks.

PANIC ATTACKS IN ANXIETY DISORDERS

Just because you experience panic attacks does not mean you have an anxiety disorder. They are, however, quite common among people with anxiety disorders, and of course, unexpected panic attacks are the central defining feature of panic disorder (APA 2000). Outside of panic disorder, panic attacks are more often expected or triggered by something in the environment. For example, someone with a specific phobia may experience a panic attack when confronted with something feared, such as a snake, an enclosed space, or a dental procedure. Someone with social anxiety disorder may experience a panic attack when in a social situation where there is the potential for criticism or negative evaluation. In PTSD, a panic attack may occur if someone encounters a reminder of a traumatic event. So, as you can see, the only real difference in panic attacks across the anxiety disorders is what brings them on. Otherwise, there really are no differences in what a panic attack feels like or its consequences. Therefore, as we present DBT skills for panic attacks, we will discuss panic attacks in more general terms, as opposed to within any particular anxiety disorder.

WHERE DO PANIC ATTACKS COME FROM?

Now, before we get into DBT skills, we want to provide just a little information on where panic attacks come from and how they develop. There are many theories on this topic, so here, we will just review a couple of the more well-supported theories.

A Biological Theory of Panic Attacks

Some people believe that panic attacks are more likely to develop among people who are predisposed to be hypersensitive to carbon dioxide levels in their bodies (Klein 1993). According to this theory, panic attacks are brought on by a part of the brain that has developed through evolution to monitor for situations where a person may be at risk of suffocation. This "monitor" in the brain sounds the alarm (that is, a panic attack) when it detects an increase in carbon dioxide levels in the bloodstream. In addition, the alarm may be activated when a person is in situations with a risk of the loss of oxygen. This would include any type of situation where a person feels trapped (for example, large crowds), or as if there is no exit or escape (McNally 1994). There is some support for (Papp, Klein, and Gorman 1993) and against (Schmidt, Telch, and Jaimez 1996) this theory. This likely means that a hypersensitivity to carbon dioxide explains why some people have panic attacks, but not others.

Psychological Theories of Panic Attacks

There are a number of psychological explanations for why panic attacks arise. However, a common underlying theme to these theories is that panic attacks come about when people negatively evaluate, or judge, the bodily sensations that often accompany anxiety or panic attacks. Basically, the idea is that some people develop beliefs that anxiety-related symptoms, such as certain thoughts or body sensations, will have negative or even catastrophic consequences, and these beliefs then actually increase their chances of having a panic attack. For example, people may believe that an increase in heart rate is a sign that they will have a heart attack. This negative (or catastrophic) evaluation of this normal bodily sensation can then lead them to fear that sensation, further increasing the intensity of that sensation and their anxiety. This spiral continues until their anxiety gets so intense that a panic attack occurs (Clark 1988).

People may also try to avoid that feared sensation—a reaction which, although understandable, usually only increases the intensity of that sensation, further fueling this vicious cycle (Tull and Roemer 2007). Beliefs that the normal bodily sensations that go along with anxiety are harmful may develop as a result of a person's upbringing or history with anxiety (Watt and Stewart 2000) or may be passed down through a person's genes and are therefore hardwired (Stein, Jang, and Livesley 1999).

FEATURES AND CONSEQUENCES OF PANIC ATTACKS

Panic attacks can be very debilitating. Next, we review some common features of panic attacks, as well as some of the negative consequences of panic attacks. At each step of the way, we also walk you through some DBT skills that may be particularly helpful in addressing that particular feature or consequence.

Avoidance

Panic attacks and avoidance go hand in hand. When people have a panic attack (whether expected or unexpected), they often go to great lengths to avoid having that experience again. People who experience expected or cued panic attacks may try to avoid cues (for example, a feared object or social situation) that could bring on a panic attack. When it comes to unexpected panic attacks in particular, people may try to avoid experiencing the bodily sensations that go along with a panic attack, such as increased heart rate and shortness of breath. For example, some people may avoid exercising, sexual activity, eating heavy meals, or drinking caffeine just to try to make sure their heart rate does not increase. People may also use substances (such as alcohol) to try to calm themselves down and lower their chances of having certain bodily sensations, such as increased heart rate and muscle tension.

These strategies may work in the short term or some of the time, but it is impossible to completely avoid bodily sensations, especially those associated with anxiety. Therefore, strategies like this just won't work. Instead, this type of avoidance often leads to a vicious cycle in which unsuccessful attempts to avoid these sensations make people try even harder to avoid them. This could eventually lead to the development of substance use or agoraphobia. Agoraphobia is a condition in which a person has intense anxiety about situations where escape or help may not be possible (for example, large crowds). As a result, a person with agoraphobia will go to great lengths to avoid these situations. Sometimes agoraphobia can become so severe that people don't feel safe outside of their homes (APA 2000).

There are a number of skills that can help you with the avoidance that accompanies panic attacks.

APPROACHING ENVIRONMENTAL CUES OF PANIC ATTACKS

One of the best skills for dealing with the avoidance found among people with panic attacks is acting opposite to the emotion (Linehan 1993b). As we discussed in chapter 4, this skill is all about helping you change emotions that may be getting in the way of your life by responding to them differently. Although fear can be a very useful emotion, providing you with important information about threats in the environment, the experience of fear in the anxiety disorders can get a bit offtrack and start to malfunction. There are few better examples of this than panic attacks.

As mentioned, panic attacks are considered a misfiring of your body's alarm system, or a false alarm. Therefore, one of the best ways to manage the fear associated with panic attacks is to approach what you fear head-on. If the situations or objects that bring about panic attacks were truly dangerous, then avoiding them would be quite helpful. The problem is that these situations and objects are not actually dangerous, and avoiding them will only make the panic worse. The best way to deal with the fear and avoidance of these cues is to approach them.

Now, we know this probably sounds incredibly counterintuitive (and really scary). Yet approaching these cues and situations provides you with the chance to learn that they are not inherently dangerous and may not always lead to a panic attack. And, if they do lead to a panic attack, it gives you the chance to learn that panic attacks themselves, although very distressing and uncomfortable, will not lead to some catastrophic outcome. Basically, you learn that you can make it through a panic attack and be okay, and you have the chance to practice other skills to help you get through the panic attack more quickly and easily.

So, how does acting opposite to fear work? Well, as we said, the basic idea is to approach what you are afraid of, over and over again. Approach any of the places, people, experiences, sensations, or activities you are afraid of, and keep approaching them until you are no longer captive to your fear. If you do this, we can guarantee that your fear of these activities and situations will decrease.

So, the first step is to identify the cues of your panic attacks that you try to avoid. Let's start first with expected or cued panic attacks. If you have any panic attacks in response to specific cues in your environment (such as certain objects or situations), or when confronted with something in the environment that you fear, use the following exercise to help you figure out how to apply the acting opposite to fear skill to these cues.

First, take some time to figure out what situations, events, or objects tend to cue your expected panic attacks.

- If you have social phobia or an intense fear of being evaluated negatively by others, cues for your panic attacks may be social in nature and may involve situations in which you think you could be judged or evaluated, such as speaking in public, eating in front of others, or being around large groups of people.

- If you have specific phobia, then the cues for your panic attacks may be specific to whatever you are afraid of, such as enclosed spaces, spiders or snakes, airplanes, or elevators.

- If you have PTSD, then the cues for your expected panic attacks may be those that remind you of your traumatic event, such as smells or sights associated with your trauma.

Take some time now to identify the environmental cues that often trigger a panic attack for you, and then write them down in the first column of exercise 8.2.

Then, for each of those situations, see if you can come up with a plan for approaching these situations or objects rather than avoiding them. Try to focus on small steps you can take to begin to approach each one, or things you can do to increase your contact with these cues. Remember, as scary as they may feel, these situations and objects are generally not actually dangerous. So, figure out a plan for beginning to approach them.

For example, if you have come to avoid crowded places because they trigger panic attacks, steps you could take to act opposite to your fear could be to go to a coffee shop at eight or nine in the morning (when it is a bit more crowded), to the mall with a friend, or to a movie theater just before the next set of movies is about to start. The goal is to keep figuring out ways to be in crowds so that you can learn that these situations are not dangerous. As another example, if you fear spiders, you could begin by going to the bookstore and looking through a book on spiders, going online and looking at pictures of spiders, renting a film that features spiders, or going to a toy store and finding a toy spider—anything to begin to approach this cue as much as possible. Now that you have the hang of it, see if you can identify three to five steps you can take to begin to approach the cues you just identified. Write these steps down in the second column.

Exercise 8.2 Identify and Manage Cues of Expected Panic Attacks

Write down all of the situations or objects in your environment that trigger expected panic attacks.	Write down up to five steps you can take to begin to approach this situation or object. Focus on small, doable actions.
	1. 2. 3. 4. 5.
	1. 2. 3. 4. 5.
	1. 2. 3. 4. 5.
	1. 2. 3. 4. 5.
	1. 2. 3. 4. 5.

	1. 2. 3. 4. 5.
	1. 2. 3. 4. 5.
	1. 2. 3. 4. 5.
	1. 2. 3. 4. 5.
	1. 2. 3. 4. 5.
	1. 2. 3. 4. 5.

Now that you have identified a plan for approaching these cues, the final step is to do it. Get started on your plan now. Remember that the more you approach these situations and objects, the less you will fear them and the less control they will have over your life. So, get going and start approaching what you fear!

We started this exercise by focusing on expected or cued panic attacks, because people often find that it's easier to identify the situations and objects outside of themselves that are a source of fear. If particular situations or objects in the environment sometimes lead to panic attacks, folks are generally aware of what these situations or objects are. They tend to be difficult to forget! For those of you who struggle with unexpected or uncued panic attacks, however, have no fear. Acting opposite to your emotion can also help with your panic attacks; it just requires a slightly different approach.

APPROACHING AVOIDED ACTIVITIES

When people have unexpected panic attacks, this means that there is nothing in particular in the environment that leads to a panic attack, no specific object or situation that they can try to avoid to prevent a panic attack. And what this means is that people who experience unexpected panic attacks often try to avoid experiencing any of the physical or bodily sensations that they associate with panic attacks, such as increased heart rate or shortness of breath.

So, what is the problem with this? Well, in addition to the fact that avoidance tends to not work in the long term, the major problem with trying to avoid these very common physical sensations is that so many different activities can make you out of breath or cause your heart rate to increase. Therefore, the only way to avoid these sensations is to severely limit your life.

Think about it: what kinds of things make your heart rate increase or cause you to be short of breath? Exercise? Walking up stairs? Seeing an exciting or scary movie? Eating or drinking something with caffeine? Having sex? And if your goal is to avoid these physical sensations, then that probably means that you need to avoid all of these activities, as well as many others. Basically, to avoid these sensations, you have to dramatically limit your life and avoid doing a ton of different activities—some of which are enjoyable and others of which are very healthy. And that can have some major downsides for your quality of life.

So, let's apply the acting opposite to fear skill to these unexpected panic attacks. The first step for this type of panic attack is to identify the physical or bodily sensations that you try to avoid, those sensations that you associate with the onset of a panic attack and that you do everything in your power not to experience. Take some time now to identify all of the bodily sensations that you try to avoid and write them down in the first column of exercise 8.3.

Next, for each of these sensations, identify the different activities that you fear could cause these sensations. Focus in particular on activities that you tend to avoid or do less of. Try to identify as many activities as possible and write them down in the second column.

Exercise 8.3 Identify Avoided Activities in Panic Attacks

Write down all of the bodily sensations associated with a panic attack that you try to avoid.	Next, write down the different activities that often lead to each of these sensations, focusing in particular on activities you try to avoid or limit.
	1. 2. 3. 4. 5.
	1. 2. 3. 4. 5.
	1. 2. 3. 4. 5.
	1. 2. 3. 4. 5.
	1. 2. 3. 4. 5.

	1. 2. 3. 4. 5.
	1. 2. 3. 4. 5.
	1. 2. 3. 4. 5.
	1. 2. 3. 4. 5.
	1. 2. 3. 4. 5.
	1. 2. 3. 4. 5.

Next, use the information from the second column of this exercise to create a list of all the activities you try to avoid because they trigger panic symptoms. Write down all of those activities in the following table. Then, see if you can, once again, come up with some small, doable steps you can take to begin to engage in these activities. How can you begin to approach these activities? Think about all of the things you can do to get into contact with these activities, focusing on small steps you can take to act opposite to your fear. Write down these steps in the second column of exercise 8.4.

Exercise 8.4 Avoid Avoidance: Manage Avoidance of Activities in Unexpected Panic Attacks

Write down all of the activities you avoid in an effort to limit your chance of having an unexpected panic attack.	Write down up to five steps you can take to begin to approach these activities. Focus on small, doable actions.
	1. 2. 3. 4. 5.
	1. 2. 3. 4. 5.
	1. 2. 3. 4. 5.
	1. 2. 3. 4. 5.

	1. 2. 3. 4. 5.
	1. 2. 3. 4. 5.
	1. 2. 3. 4. 5.
	1. 2. 3. 4. 5.
	1. 2. 3. 4. 5.
	1. 2. 3. 4. 5.

Congratulations! Now that you have identified the steps you can take to approach these activities and address your avoidance, you are one step closer to breaking free of panic attacks and their hold on your life. This is a really big step. We know it can be difficult to break the cycle of avoidance, so even taking the time to identify what you can do to approach these activities can be really scary. And yet, this is also the first step on the road to recovery. The next step is to begin to make your way through this list, doing one thing at a time to approach these activities.

APPROACHING THE BODILY SENSATIONS ASSOCIATED WITH PANIC ATTACKS

Another way to address the avoidance that goes along with panic attacks is to approach the very sensations associated with panic attacks. The exercises so far have focused on helping you manage avoidance of situations, objects, and activities. One reason for this is that the avoidance of these activities and situations can be problematic in and of itself, interfering with your quality of life and limiting your ability to live your life fully. Most of these forms of avoidance, however, are really all about avoiding the bodily sensations that go along with panic attacks. Isn't that one of the main reasons you avoid so many of the activities and situations you identified previously? For many people, the avoidance of these bodily sensations is what drives the rest of their avoidance behaviors. So, the best way to address this form of avoidance is to approach these sensations themselves. And, as much as that may be a very scary proposition, there are DBT skills to help you through it.

Two skills in particular can be very helpful. The first is to use the acting opposite to emotion skill (Linehan 1993b) we described previously to approach each of the feared bodily sensations you identified in exercise 8.3. Use the following exercise to help you with this. First, write down again in the first column all of the bodily sensations you associate with panic attacks and try to avoid. They will be the same sensations you identified in exercise 8.3.

Exercise 8.5 How to Approach Feared Bodily Sensations Associated with Panic Attacks

Write down all of the bodily sensations associated with a panic attack that you try to avoid.	Next, write down different things you could do or actions you could take that could lead to these sensations and put you into contact with them.
	1. 2. 3. 4. 5.

	1. 2. 3. 4. 5.
	1. 2. 3. 4. 5.
	1. 2. 3. 4. 5.
	1. 2. 3. 4. 5.
	1. 2. 3. 4. 5.
	1. 2. 3. 4. 5.

Next, identify several different things you could do to get in touch with these bodily sensations. Try to generate as many actions as possible that could lead to these sensations and put you into contact with these internal experiences. They don't have to be normal activities you would typically do in your everyday life, just anything that could give you the chance to approach these feared sensations. So, if you are afraid of your heart racing, think of things you can do to get your blood pumping. How about jumping up and down, running up stairs, or doing push-ups? See table 8.1 for different ideas about how to get into contact with the physical sensations that often go along with panic attacks (Schmidt and Trakowski 2004). Once you have identified actions you think may work for you, write them in the second column of exercise 8.5. Use this list to help you get in contact with these sensations, approaching them over and over again until they become less scary.

Table 8.1 Increasing Contact with Bodily Sensations

Activity	Bodily sensations that may arise from the activity
1. Shaking your head	Dizziness Light-headedness
2. Placing your head between your knees	Pressure and tension in your head Dizziness Light-headedness
3. Running in place, or up and down stairs	Shortness of breath Rapid heartbeat Muscle tension Sweating Light-headedness
4. Holding your breath	Shortness of breath Light-headedness Tension or pain in chest
5. Spinning around in a chair	Dizziness Light-headedness Nausea Blurred vision Headache

6. Breathing through a straw	Shortness of breath Choking sensations Rapid heartbeat Dizziness Light-headedness Headache
7. Hyperventilating	Dizziness Tingling in your hands Light-headedness Rapid heartbeat Tension or pain in chest Shortness of breath Dry mouth Shaking or trembling
8. Doing push-ups	Muscle tension Shaking or trembling Rapid heartbeat

Another set of skills that can help you approach these feared bodily sensations is the DBT mindfulness skills (Linehan 1993b). As we mentioned in chapter 3, the mindfulness skills in DBT can help you get in contact with internal experiences (such as thoughts, feelings, and physical sensations) that you may often try to avoid. And, because mindfulness skills are not just about what to do but how to do it, these skills can help you get in touch with these sensations in a way that will be beneficial to you.

Specifically, you can use the DBT skill of noticing your experience without judging it (Linehan 1993b) to help you begin to approach the bodily sensations associated with panic attacks. The first part of this skill simply involves noticing your internal experience without getting caught up in or reacting to it. So, rather than reacting to your bodily sensations or getting caught up in them, you would make it your goal in using this skill to just notice each sensation as it arises, without trying to push it away or cling to it. Simply focus all of your attention on observing any bodily sensations you experience, watching them arise and pass from one moment to the next.

The second part of this skill involves the particular way in which we want you to practice observing these sensations. Specifically, as you practice noticing your bodily sensations and observing them as they arise and pass, make sure that you take a nonevaluative stance. Allow yourself to notice these sensations without judging or evaluating them. Focus on just noticing each sensation as it is, rather than judging it as bad or wrong. Keep in mind that these bodily sensations are simply a natural part of being alive, and something that every human being experiences. Observing your experiences in this way will help you connect with the fact that these sensations are not inherently dangerous or problematic, and will go a long way in helping you stop avoiding these sensations.

The following exercise provides some simple step-by-step instructions for noticing your bodily sensations without judgment or evaluation. Try it out and see how it works!

Exercise 8.6 Practice Nonjudgmentally Noticing Your Bodily Sensations

1. To begin, find a comfortable and quiet place where you can sit or lie down.

2. Close your eyes.

3. Focus your attention on your breathing. Notice what it feels like to breathe in and out. Notice what parts of your body move as you breathe in and out.

4. Expand your awareness outward to different parts of your body (for example, your legs, arms, back, or neck). Basically, bring your attention to parts of your body where you often feel tension or experience feared bodily sensations.

5. Do not label or judge those sensations, but instead try to notice them as just sensations, nothing else.

6. If you notice that you are labeling or judging those sensations, notice that evaluation or thought, and then return your attention to noticing the sensations as just sensations.

7. If you get distracted by judgments or thoughts, your job is just to notice that and then return your attention to nonjudgmentally noticing your sensations every time.

8. Practice focusing your awareness on different parts of your body. Move your attention across your entire body, focusing on observing a variety of different bodily sensations without judging or evaluating them.

9. Practice this exercise for at least fifteen minutes a couple of times a day. Initially, make sure you practice this exercise at times when you don't feel overly anxious. This will make it easier to establish a new habit of noticing your experience without judgment.

Catastrophic Beliefs about or Misinterpretations of Bodily Sensations

As mentioned, panic attacks sometimes come about when people evaluate certain bodily sensations as negative in some way. For example, some people who experience certain anxiety-related bodily sensations may believe that they are going crazy, dying, or about to lose control. They may misinterpret these very normal bodily sensations as a sign of impending doom. And it is these interpretations that then actually increase the chance of having a panic attack. Think about it: if you believe that your racing heart is a sign that you are about to have a heart attack, will you feel better, or will you become even more anxious and afraid? We would guess the latter. And that makes a lot of sense. If these sensations really were a sign that you were about to die or were having a heart attack, then wouldn't that level of fear make sense? Of course! The problem is that these beliefs, while understandable, are not necessarily true or accurate. So, buying into them and believing that they are 100 percent true may not be incredibly helpful. The good news, though, is that you don't have to change these beliefs or keep yourself from thinking this way to move forward in your recovery. Instead, there is a really useful DBT skill that can help with these types of thoughts.

OBJECTIVELY LABELING YOUR EXPERIENCE AS WHAT IT IS

One of the best skills for dealing with these types of thoughts is the DBT skill of objectively labeling your experience (Linehan 1993b). The purpose of this skill is to acknowledge and describe your experience as what it is, labeling a feeling as just a feeling, a sensation as just a sensation, and a thought as just a thought. So, the next time you find yourself experiencing some of the bodily sensations that accompany panic attacks, begin by labeling that experience objectively and putting it into words. For example, say to yourself *My heart is beginning to beat faster*, *My breathing is becoming more shallow*, or *I'm having the sensation of shortness of breath*. Then (and this is the important piece), if you notice any thoughts associated with that experience, make sure to label those thoughts as just thoughts. For example, rather than believing *I'm having a heart attack* or *I'm about to die*, describe these thoughts as just thoughts by saying in your mind *The thought "I'm having a heart attack" has come into my mind* or *The thought "I'm about to die" has just entered my mind*. Approaching your thoughts in this way and clearly labeling them as they are—just thoughts that your mind has generated—will help you take a step back from these thoughts and not buy into them as if they were literally true.

The following exercise may help with this. You can think about it as a way of making this mindfulness skill more concrete. To begin, think about all of the different thoughts you have when you experience a panic attack. Try to focus on those thoughts that are most catastrophic and that you generally buy into and accept as reality. Then, write those thoughts in the following exercise. This will help you connect with the fact that this type of thinking is simply the activity of the mind.

Exercise 8.7 Label Your Thoughts as Just Thoughts

Use this worksheet to identify thoughts associated with your panic attacks. Write down all of the thoughts that accompany your panic attacks. When you are writing them, focus on connecting with the first part of the sentence and the fact that they are just thoughts.

I am having the thought that _____

_____.

I am having the thought that _____

_____.

I am having the thought that _____

_____.

I am having the thought that _____

_____.

I am having the thought that _____

_____.

I am having the thought that _____

_____.

I am having the thought that _____

_____.

I am having the thought that _____

_____.

I am having the thought that _____

_____.

Increased Attention toward Bodily Sensations

One of the other features of panic attacks that can unfortunately increase your chance of having future panic attacks is the tendency to pay much greater attention to your bodily sensations than do people who don't have panic attacks. This is called *having hypervigilance toward bodily sensations*, and it generally happens because people are so afraid of having another panic attack that they are constantly on guard for any sensation that could be a sign that a panic attack may occur. Basically, many people with panic attacks spend a lot of time scanning their bodies and focusing on their bodily sensations to make sure that they can catch the first sign of an impending panic attack. For example, people who struggle with panic attacks may find that they are constantly scanning their bodies to see if they can detect any small change in heart rate or breathing. Now, in some ways, this makes a lot of sense. It is one way of trying to establish a sense of control and predictability over something that can feel so out of control and unpredictable. And, who wouldn't want to have more control over when panic attacks occur? The problem, though, is that the more you pay attention to these types of bodily sensations, the more likely you will be to notice these sensations at very low levels—far below those that should normally concern you. And, as we discussed, the more likely you are to notice them, the more likely you may be to try to avoid them. Therefore, as much as we understand the desire to be more aware of these sensations and as much as we believe that awareness of internal experiences is often a really healthy and adaptive thing, in this case this level of increased awareness will probably only increase your risk of having more panic attacks.

So, the best bet is to try to learn some skills for broadening your awareness to include aspects of your experience beyond just these bodily sensations. And, as you may have guessed, DBT has some really useful skills that can help you with this.

NOTICING AND LABELING SENSORY INFORMATION

One of the best ways to broaden your awareness beyond just your bodily sensations is to use the DBT skills of noticing and labeling your experience (Linehan 1993b) to focus your attention on your external environment and your sensory information. So, rather than limiting your awareness to just your bodily sensations, expand that awareness to notice all of the information coming through your senses. Focus on each of your five senses: taste, touch, smell, hearing, and sight. See if you can focus all of your attention on one sense at a time, noticing everything that is coming through that particular sensory channel. Remember not to judge these experiences as good or bad, but just focus on the senses and everything you are experiencing in the moment. See if you can then begin to label these experiences, putting this sensory information into words and focusing on being as descriptive as possible. Ask yourself the following questions.

Exercise 8.8 Questions to Help You Notice and Label Sensory Information

Ask yourself these questions to help you get in touch with and describe your sensory experiences.

Taste:

What do I taste right now?

Where do I first notice this taste in my mouth?

Is it subtle or strong?

Is it bitter, sweet, or salty?

Is it cold or hot?

How long does the taste last?

Touch:

What do I feel against my skin?

What do I feel against my fingertips?

What textures do I feel?

Is what I am feeling soft or hard?

Is it rough or smooth?

Is it warm or cool to the touch?

Smell:

What scents do I notice?

Are they strong or mild?

How does the scent change over time?

How long does the scent last?

Sound:

What do I hear right now?

Are the sounds nearby or far away?

Are they loud or soft?

Is their pitch high or low?

How long does each sound last?

Sight:

What do I see right now?

What objects do I observe?

What colors do I notice?

What textures and patterns do I see?

What shapes do I see?

Focusing on your external environment will help broaden your attention beyond just your bodily sensations, keeping you from getting too caught up in these sensations. Try this the next time you find yourself drawn to only your bodily sensations and see how helpful it can be.

MOVING FORWARD

In this chapter, we gave you a lot of information on panic attacks and how they develop. We also taught you a number of different skills that you can use to manage panic attacks. Take some time to practice all of the different skills presented in this chapter and see what works best for you. You may find that some of these skills work better than others, or that some work only in certain situations or at certain times. This is incredibly important information to have, and the only way to get this information is to practice these skills regularly. It is also important to be patient with both yourself and the skills. Reducing avoidance behaviors and increasing contact with feared bodily sensations can be a very frightening experience. The more you do so, however, the easier it will become, and the more you will notice a reduction in your panic attacks. So, try these skills and start moving down the road to breaking free of the control that panic attacks can have on your life!

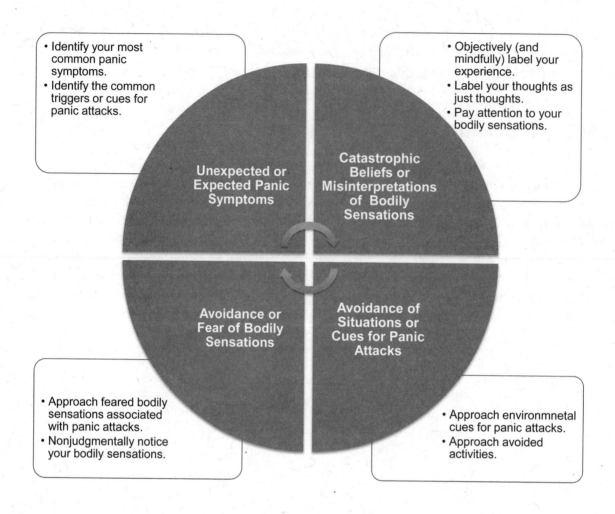

- Identify your most common panic symptoms.
- Identify the common triggers or cues for panic attacks.

- Objectively (and mindfully) label your experience.
- Label your thoughts as just thoughts.
- Pay attention to your bodily sensations.

Unexpected or Expected Panic Symptoms

Catastrophic Beliefs or Misinterpretations of Bodily Sensations

Avoidance or Fear of Bodily Sensations

Avoidance of Situations or Cues for Panic Attacks

- Approach feared bodily sensations associated with panic attacks.
- Nonjudgmentally notice your bodily sensations.

- Approach environmnetal cues for panic attacks.
- Approach avoided activities.

Figure 8.1   **Putting It All Together: DBT Skills to Manage Panic Symptoms**

CHAPTER 9

Obsessions and Compulsive Behaviors

You may have noticed the growing number of television programs that feature characters who have the anxiety disorder obsessive-compulsive disorder (OCD). These shows depict people who struggle with a unique kind of anxiety-provoking intrusive thought and engage in a variety of behaviors that might seem very odd, such as complusive hand washing, counting, or hoarding.

These programs show extreme examples of obsessions and compulsions. However, you might be surprised to learn that less-extreme obsessions and compulsions are actually fairly common among people in general. In several chapters we discussed how people commonly experience several anxiety symptoms (such as worry and panic attacks) even if they don't have an anxiety disorder. The same goes for obsessions and compulsions. In fact, studies have found that up to 90 percent of the general population experience obsessive thoughts and compulsions (Rachman and de Silva 1978; Salkovskis and Harrison 1984). Some people might have minor intrusive thoughts about leaving the stove on, losing a wallet, or locking the front door. As a result, they may check the stove, their pocket, or the front door several times just to ensure that everything is safe. These thoughts and behaviors may take up some time, but in the end, they don't really interfere with a person's life. Some people, however, develop frequent, intense, and incredibly distressing obsessive thoughts and compulsions that greatly interfere with their lives. We will focus our attention on those symptoms here.

OBSESSIONS AND COMPULSIONS

Obsessions are recurrent and persistent thoughts that are viewed as intrusive (that is, coming up unexpectedly), unwanted, and inappropriate. These thoughts also bring up considerable amounts of anxiety and distress. In fact, obsessions can be so distressing that they even bring on panic attacks (Steketee and Barlow 2002). In addition to thoughts, obsessions can also take the form of impulses (intense desires or urges to engage in some kind of behavior) and images that unexpectedly come into a person's mind (APA 2000). In exercise 9.1, we provide some common obsessions (Baer 2000; Steketee and Barlow 2002). Obsessions can really be about anything, so this is not an exhaustive list, but it might give you some idea of the different types of obsessions that can develop. Check off any that you experience. You can also provide some of your own if they are not on the list. In completing this list, keep in mind the definition of obsessions that we provided previously. As we will discuss, it is actually quite common to have some of these thoughts from time to time. Focus instead on thoughts that are persistent, distressing, and intense and that interfere with your life.

Exercise 9.1 What Are Your Obsessions About?

Mark all that apply.

	Fears about being exposed to germs or dirt
	Concerns about being exposed to bodily fluids that may transmit certain illnesses (for example, HIV, hepatitis C)
	Concerns about having or developing a particular disease (for example, cancer)
	Concerns about eating food that could be contaminated, leading to illness or an allergic reaction
	Concerns about being exposed to environmental toxins (for example, radiation, lead)
	Fears that you might accidentally or impulsively physically harm yourself in some way
	Concerns that you will do something to either accidentally or impulsively hurt someone else
	Fears that you might be unable to control your behavior in front of others (for example, shouting out swear words, writing rude comments in an e-mail)
	Blasphemous thoughts (for example, lewd or angry thoughts toward some religious figure)
	Fears of being possessed by some evil force
	Thoughts about sexual acts that are illegal, looked down on, or considered lewd (may include concerns about acting on these thoughts)
	Concerns about sexual orientation even though you have no reason to doubt your sexual orientation

	Fears of death or dying, or of doing something to bring on another person's death
	Desires for symmetry and order (this may include things in your environment and how you appear to others)
	Concerns about not being perfect in your speech or writing (for example, having to say or write things the "right" way)
	Anxiety about throwing away or losing something of value
	Fears of losing another person, such as your child
	Doubting your actions (for example, doubting that you turned the iron off even when you remember having done so)
	Extreme difficulties in making a decision for fear of making the wrong choice
	Fears related to superstitions (for example, breaking a mirror, crossing the path of a black cat, needing to knock on wood)
	Believing that certain objects, colors, numbers, or images convey significant information about something that will or could happen

Do you have other obsessions? List them.

1.

2.

3.

4.

5.

6.

7.

8.

"Compulsions" can refer to behaviors or mental activities that occur in response to an obsession. People often feel that they have no choice when it comes to compulsions. They may feel driven to engage in some kind of compulsion. Compulsions may be viewed as rules that have to be followed to avoid severe consequences (APA 2000). Compulsions are intimately tied to obsessions. They are a way of neutralizing obsessions or relieving anxiety stemming from an obsession. For example, a person who has an obsessive thought that they might accidentally throw away or lose something of sentimental value may not throw away anything. This may include things that the person logically knows don't have sentimental value, such as newspapers, grocery bags, and food containers. This type of compulsive behavior (hoarding) helps alleviate any anxiety stemming from the possibility that something of sentimental value might be accidentally thrown away.

In exercise 9.2, we provide a list of compulsions that people can experience (Baer 2000; Steketee and Barlow 2002). As with obsessions, we want you to focus on those compulsions that result in considerable distress and interfere with your life. Don't include compulsions that occur infrequently or are easy to resist.

Exercise 9.2 What Kind of Compulsions Do You Experience?

Mark all that apply.

	Excessive hand washing, bathing, showering, or grooming
	Excessive cleaning of your house or other valued objects (for example, your car)
	Behaviors focused on preventing contamination (for example, wearing gloves, not touching doorknobs or mail, refusing to use public restrooms)
	Frequent and persistent checking of locks, appliances, alarm systems, and so on
	Checking your body or someone else's to make sure you did not harm it
	Frequent checking to make sure you did not make a mistake on something, such as homework or bills
	Repetition of basic activities, such as turning a light switch on and off over and over again
	Needing to do things in a certain order or a certain number of times (for example, having to touch a door five times before opening or closing it)
	The need to repeatedly go through an entry, such as walking through a doorway or entering a building over and over again
	Extreme organizing behavior to make sure everything is perfectly aligned or in perfect order
	Counting (for example, counting floor tiles or other objects in your environment)
	Having to do certain behaviors in a certain order, such as when getting dressed in the morning, preparing a meal, or eating a meal
	Excessive religious activities, such as praying
	Repetition of certain phrases or words when talking or reading

	Seeking constant reassurance
	Saving items that you do not really need (such as newspapers and mail)
	Collecting items that you find or come across, such as pieces of glass that you find on the street
	Having to do something over and over again until you feel that you've done it "just right"
	Needing to touch certain objects
	Repeated behaviors stemming from superstitions (such as knocking on wood)
	Needing to bring up certain thoughts or engage in other mental activities to counter bad thoughts (for example, mentally reciting a poem or stating some phrase)

Do you have other compulsions? List them.

1.

2.

3.

4.

5.

6.

7.

8.

Now that you have a better understanding of the types of obsessions and compulsions you experience, let's briefly talk about the anxiety disorder that these symptoms are a part of.

OBSESSIVE-COMPULSIVE DISORDER

In OCD, a person experiences obsessions, compulsions, or both as defined previously. In addition, people with OCD try to ignore, stop, or push down their obsessions. The obsessions are also viewed as a product of the person's own mind. That is, people with OCD know that their minds produce these thoughts or images. People with OCD also recognize that their obsessions, compulsions, or both are excessive and unrealistic. Finally, to be diagnosed with OCD, the symptoms need to result in high levels of anxiety and distress, as well as greatly interfere with a person's life (APA 2000). This last criterion is not too hard to meet. If you look back at the obsessions and compulsions we listed previously, you can see how these activities may take up a substantial portion of someone's day, greatly interfering with relationships, school, or the ability to work. As a result, OCD can have a tremendous negative impact on a person's life. In fact, OCD is one anxiety disorder that has a high likelihood of leading to the experience of severe negative consequences, such as hospitalization or the development of other disorders, such as depression (Steketee and Barlow 2002).

IS IT AN OBSESSION, WORRY, OR REEXPERIENCING?

If you have looked through other chapters in this book, you might have noticed that there is quite a bit of overlap among the different symptoms of anxiety. This is definitely the case when it comes to obsessions. Obsessions are intrusive and repetitive thoughts, just like worry and the reexperiencing symptoms of PTSD. However, you can distinguish obsessions from other anxiety symptoms by the content of your intrusive thoughts.

Obsessions are often composed of unrealistic, bizarre, and strange thoughts. They may even seem foreign to you, kind of as if they don't really belong in your head. For example, a mother may have the thought that she will smother her baby. This thought may come up even though she has absolutely no desire to do so or reason to believe that she will. Worry, on the other hand, is often made up of thoughts that are more realistic (even if the events in those thoughts are somewhat exaggerated or unlikely to occur in the future) and consistent with people's views of themselves, their lives, or both. For example, people might worry about keeping their jobs or paying their bills in the future. These concerns are much more realistic and logical than the mother's obsession about her baby. Finally, intrusive thoughts seen in PTSD are exclusively focused on the traumatic event that was experienced.

WHY DO OBSESSIONS AND COMPULSIONS DEVELOP?

Just like some of the other symptoms of anxiety that we discussed, such as worry, obsessions and compulsions (as strange as they might seem) do serve some kind of purpose. In actuality, the world can be a dangerous place, and to some degree, we are always at risk of some kind of harm. For some people, the uncontrollability and unpredictability of life and all of its unknown dangers is very difficult to tolerate. This may be particularly true for someone who has experienced a traumatic or very stressful life event, a situation that often increases fears of uncontrollability and unpredictability. In fact, there is some evidence that OCD may develop after such events (Cromer, Schmidt, and Murphy 2007). Obsessions and compulsions develop in an attempt to establish some sense of controllability, predictability, certainty, and safety.

For example, let's say that a mother frequently involuntarily imagines her child dying from drinking some household cleanser. Obviously, this image will be quite distressing, and even if the probability of its happening is very low, the mother, of course, will be motivated to make sure it doesn't happen because, even with the very low chance that it could happen, she doesn't want to risk it. Therefore, she engages in some compulsive behavior to make sure her child is safe. She may constantly check the caps of cleansers to make sure they are secure. She may organize cleansers in a certain way so that the more harmful ones are out of her child's reach. She may also frequently check on her child to make sure he is okay and has not ingested anything. All of these actions provide a feeling of control and predictability, reducing her anxiety. The problem is that these feelings of reassurance are fleeting. The image will probably keep popping into her head, increasing her need to engage in certain compulsions.

Before we move on to specific DBT skills for obsessions and compulsions, it is important to understand how your obsessions and compulsions work together. In exercise 9.3, we would like you to write down some obsessions that you have. Look back to exercise 9.1 if you need help identifying some. Then, identify the behavior or mental act that occurs in response to the obsession. Use exercise 9.2 if you need some help identifying specific compulsions. Being more aware of how your obsessions and compulsions work together will help you identify ways in which you can break that connection and come up with healthier and more effective ways of managing the anxiety that comes from your obsessions.

Exercise 9.3 What Compulsions Follow Your Obsessions?

Obsessions	Compulsions

FEATURES AND CONSEQUENCES OF OBSESSIONS AND COMPULSIONS

As you might expect, obsessions and compulsions can have a major impact on a person's life. Next, we describe some of the features and negative consequences of obsessions and compulsions. We also present some specific DBT skills that may help you manage your obsessions and compulsions.

The content of obsessions is incredibly distressing and anxiety provoking. As a result, when obsessive thoughts or images come into your mind, they will quickly grab your attention. In addition, once you notice the obsessive thought or image, your anxiety will increase, which will make the obsession intensify. This cycle will continue until you engage in some kind of action to push down or neutralize the obsession. However, as we mentioned previously, this will be effective only in the short term, and in the long term, it will just cause those obsessions to keep coming up.

In addition, some people with OCD buy into their obsessions so much that they believe that having a thought about some kind of behavior is the same as engaging in that behavior. For example, let's say that the thought or image frequently comes into a man's mind that he will hurt his dog. Even though he has never hurt his dog and would never want to, for him, having this thought is just as bad as actually hurting his dog. As a result, in addition to anxiety and fear, he experiences considerable guilt and shame. This is called *thought-action fusion* (Berle and Starcevic 2005). Basically, the thought is fused or becomes one with the actual behavior.

Mindfully Noticing and Labeling a Thought as a Thought

One way to counteract this problem of getting stuck in your obsessions is to step back in your mind and see your thoughts for what they are, just thoughts. When you take a mindful perspective on the activity of your mind, thoughts are simply thoughts, no more and no less. Just having a thought doesn't mean that you have to act on it or that you will act on it at some point. Thoughts and actions are two different things. We all have many different types of thoughts that we never act on. Think of how many times you've been attracted to someone you have seen in a public place and thought of asking that person out. How many of those times did you just walk up to the person and ask? Maybe you did this some of the time, but probably not every time. Similarly, think of all the times you have had strong cravings for or thoughts about a particular type of food. There are times when you acted on your thoughts or cravings and other times when you did not. So, remember that a thought is just a thought, even if it feels powerful, compelling, and important, as obsessions often do.

Exercise 9.4 Mindfully Notice Your Thoughts

There are many ways to mindfully step back and notice your thoughts. Here are a few that you can practice. At first, we recommend that you practice these strategies in a quiet place where nobody will bother you, when you feel relatively relaxed. Also, the first time you practice these strategies, it may be best to do so with thoughts that are going through your mind at the time, but not with obsessive thoughts. This is because it's often best to give yourself an easier task when you are first practicing a new skill, rather than to expect yourself to use the skill effectively when it's most difficult (when you feel consumed by obsessive thoughts). Over time, you will find that you can employ the strategy much more easily and automatically, just as over time, the behaviors involved in driving with a stick shift become nearly "automatic."

1. This exercise involves you imagining your thoughts on train cars and watching them roll by (McKay et al. 2007). If you are good at using your imagination and visualizing, then this might be a useful way for

you to practice. This exercise works best with your eyes closed. Imagine that you are sitting on the side of a small, grassy hill. The sun is shining outside, the birds are chirping in a nearby tree, and you see dandelions and daffodils throughout the grass. Do your best to jump into this scene in your imagination and experience all of the sights, sounds, textures, and smells that you notice. Below you, about thirty feet away, is a train track. Watch the train as it goes by. Imagine that it is going by at about medium to slow speed, not too fast for you to see the individual cars, but not too slow either. Whenever you notice a thought going through your mind, see if you can imagine it written on one of the train cars as the train goes by. Imagine that each train car is one of your thoughts. Whenever a thought enters your mind, just "see" it on the train car as it goes by. Watch the thought, or train car, glide on by, and then look at the next one and see what thought you see on that one. Don't jump on the thought train; just let it continue to go by. If you notice no thoughts, then just observe blank train cars with nothing written on them. But then, if you have a thought about having no thoughts (*Hey, I'm not having any thoughts*), put that thought on the next train car and watch it too. Remind yourself that a thought is just a thought. You can step back and notice it without acting on it. You can do this imagery exercise with train cars, clouds floating by in the sky, leaves on a stream, helium balloons floating up into the sky, or whatever works best for you. Also, if you have trouble seeing the written thoughts on the train cars or the clouds, then just imagine that you see a train car with nothing written on it (or a cloud) each time you have a thought, and then watch it pass on by. The people we have worked with have found this quite helpful and have had all sorts of creative ideas about how to use this strategy, so we hope that you find it helpful too.

2. Another way to practice mindfulness of your thoughts is to categorize them. If you have trouble visualizing, then this strategy might be the best one for you. But, even if you are adept at visualizing things, this is still quite a helpful strategy. You can do this exercise with your eyes open or closed. The first thing to do is to stop and notice the thoughts going through your mind. Whenever you notice a thought, stop yourself there, pay attention to the thought, and then categorize it. Find a category in which to put the thought. For example, if you had the thought *I'm hungry; I wonder what I'll make for dinner*, you could say to yourself *Thought about dinner*. If you had the thought *I wonder if I checked the lock on the door before I left*, you could say to yourself *Thought about the door*, and so on. Just keep stopping with each thought you have, find an appropriate (but very brief) category for it, and then step back and wait for other thoughts. Many people find that this strategy helps calm their minds and that they feel a lot less wrapped up or stuck in their thoughts the more they practice it. Here's an example using thoughts one of us had while sitting in a library:

I'm in the library; I wonder if people think it's weird that my eyes are closed as I sit in front of my computer.	*Thought about how I look.*
Why is that woman wearing gloves while she carries a footstool around the library?	*Thought about a person.*
It's snowing outside.	*Thought about the weather.*

I'm hungry; I wonder if I can eat my snack without anyone noticing that I'm eating in the library.	*Thought about food.*
That poor girl can't find a seat to work in.	*Thought about a person.*

Exercise 9.5 Mindfully Notice the Sensations of the Moment

Another way to disentangle yourself from your thoughts is to step back and mindfully pay attention to and notice all of the sensations of the present moment. This might be an easier strategy to use than in exercise 9.1 when your thoughts are overwhelming. The idea here is to basically jump out of your head and into your current surroundings. When you catch yourself getting all tangled up in your thoughts (obsessive or otherwise), immediately step back from your thoughts, tell yourself *I'm obsessing*, and redirect your attention outward to the things around you, using all of your five senses. Start with sight. Look around you and notice what you see. Then, label and describe what you see, using the following table. Do the same with smell. Focus on your nose and any sensations of smell that you might be experiencing. Really zero in with your attention, like a laser beam, on the sensations of smell, and then use words to label or describe what you noticed. Move on to hearing, and to touch and taste as well, doing the exact same thing. Keep your mind anchored in your external environment, and whenever your thoughts start to pull you back, gently guide your mind back to your surroundings.

Another way to practice redirecting your attention to sensations is to purposely create sensations for yourself to focus on. For example, you could use some of the *self-soothing* strategies discussed in chapter 3 to produce soothing or calming sensations of sight, sound, touch, taste, or hearing, and then notice and label those experiences. The main idea is to get yourself out of your head and into your experiences of the present moment.

Exercise 9.6 Label and Describe the Sensations of the Moment

Sight	

Smell	
Sound	
Touch	
Taste	

Resisting Compulsions

One major way to reduce the frequency and power of obsessions is by resisting the urge to engage in compulsions. In the short term only, compulsions help to alleviate anxiety associated with obsessions. By engaging in a compulsion, however, you are also verifying that the obsession was true or valid, increasing the likelihood that it will come up again. Therefore, it is very important to identify ways to resist urges to engage in some kind of compulsion.

Exercise 9.7 Steps to Take to Resist Compulsions

If you suffer from OCD, one of the most important things, and one of the hardest things, you can do for yourself is to resist compulsions. People have likely told you, "Why don't you just resist the urge to check the door ten times, to wash your hands, or to (perform whatever other ritualistic or neutralizing compulsions you might have)?" What people don't realize is that it's almost like asking someone who is starving to resist the urge to eat a delectable pizza that is right within reach. Resisting compulsions is not easily done, but fortunately we have some tips for you, and with these DBT strategies, you might find that you become better and better able to avoid compulsive behavior. In doing so, you are taking a big step on the path to recovery.

1. The first step is to identify the urge or desire to act, to perform the compulsion. To do this, you have to use your mindfulness skills to notice and get familiar with how you feel when you have the desire to do compulsive behaviors. For some people, it's a feeling of uneasiness in the chest or abdomen, a feeling of things crawling on your skin, a sense of being "pushed" to do something, a feeling of doom or anxiety that something terrible has happened or will happen, and so on. Get familiar with what you feel like when you want to do a compulsive behavior.

2. The next step is to remind yourself that with compulsive behavior, any fear or anxiety you feel probably is what we would call a "false alarm." This means that whatever you're afraid might happen if you don't do the compulsive behavior probably won't happen at all. It's highly unlikely that you actually forgot to lock the door, ran over someone in the street, will contract a terrible illness from touching a doorknob, or will be subject to eternal torment in hell because you cursed. Your mind might try to convince you: *Well, you never know. How can I know for sure? What if I didn't lock the door, or what if God is angry with me? How do we ever know for sure? I might as well just do the neutralizing or compulsive behavior just in case.* The problem is that with particular obsessions and compulsions, we really don't know for sure. In this case, you have to practice *acceptance* of the uncertainty factor, and just let these thoughts occur without acting on them.

3. The next step is to use *opposite action* by doing the opposite (or something close to it) of what you feel like doing. If you have contamination- or germ-related obsessions and compulsively wash your hands after you touch doorknobs, then the idea would be to seek out and touch as many doorknobs as possible without washing your hands. This might be a tall order at first, so perhaps just start by telling yourself to stay away from all places where you could wash your hands, and purposely avoid hand washing. Similarly, if you're driving and think you might have run something or someone over, just keep driving, even though it's the last thing you want to do and your whole mind and body are screaming at you to go back and check. The same thing goes for the desire to engage in "checking" behaviors (checking your door and so on) and for religious compulsions, which often involve neutralizing "bad" things you might have done or said. For religious compulsions, let's say you took the Lord's name in vain, swore, or wore a shirt with "profanity" on it. The opposite action would be to purposely do this over and over again without any corrective or neutralizing actions.

4. The next step is to *immerse yourself mindfully* in whatever activity you are doing in the moment. If you have done the opposite action, and now you're walking or driving to work, making food, or talking with someone, your job is to simply throw yourself into whatever activity you are currently engaged in. Let that activity be your whole world in that moment. If obsessive thoughts or urges to engage in compulsive actions start creeping in, just notice them, and keep throwing your mind back into whatever you're doing. Immersing yourself in your current activity is one of the best ways to fill up your brain so that there's less room for obsessions and compulsions to enter.

5. If you are having a very hard time doing any of this, then use *distraction* strategies to get your mind occupied and to resist the urge to engage in compulsive behavior. By your resisting a compulsion, your anxiety will increase considerably. In addition, the obsession might get stronger or worse. As a result, you will feel a very strong urge to engage in some kind of compulsion. Distraction, as we've mentioned, is one of the distress tolerance skills, and it turns out to be one of the best ways to avoid acting on impulses or urges. Get your mind busy with distracting activities that fill up your brain so that there's little room left for your compulsions or obsessions. Do a crossword or sudoku, have a stimulating conversation with someone, eat strongly flavored food, work out vigorously at the gym, go for a run, or do some other activity that grabs your attention. Keep doing it until the urge to act on the compulsion is a little weaker and more manageable, and then do steps 2, 3, and 4.

- *Michael's Story*

Michael, aged forty-three, had a long history of OCD, starting from middle childhood. He also struggled with social anxiety disorder. When he came to see one of us, he had been through several intensive hospital-based treatments for OCD and had learned a lot about how to manage his symptoms. He also was extremely well read on the subject, having explored many books on OCD and self-help books to better understand his difficulties. He came to one of us specifically because he thought that DBT skills might help him in some ways that his other treatments had not yet helped him. When he first came in for therapy, he explained that he had obsessive thoughts and images that involved jamming his toothbrush into his gums and cheeks whenever he brushed his teeth. He was afraid that he might seriously harm himself and, as a result, avoided brushing his teeth or used very soft or very wide toothbrushes that were less likely to harm him. When he began to learn mindfulness skills, he found that the most helpful skill was that of simply *immersing and throwing himself into* the act of brushing his teeth. He threw his whole mind into this activity, despite his frequent obsession and images about jabbing the toothbrush into his mouth. After several weeks of purposely brushing his teeth whenever he felt the urge to avoid doing so (*opposite action*), and mindfully throwing himself into the activity, he found that the obsessions became less frequent and intense and turned into only occasional, fleeting thoughts.

Michael also had difficulty with religious obsessions and compulsions. For example, he once bought a shirt with a famous singer on it, and when he found out that this singer was an anarchist, he had obsessive thoughts that God would punish him for wearing such a shirt. As you can probably guess, the solution to this problem involved Michael's *acting opposite* to his urges to neutralize (say prayers to set things right) and to get rid of the shirt. In fact, opposite action in this case involved Michael's wearing the shirt and saying things that he thought would displease God, and avoiding the urge to pray or neutralize anything he said. Over several months of his practicing these and other skills, Michael found himself much freer from the religious compulsions and obsessions and, as a result, much freer to focus on what was really important to him, such as establishing meaningful relationships and getting a job.

MOVING FORWARD

The world can be a scary place, so it makes sense that you would want to feel safe or that you would want your loved ones to be safe. This is human and perfectly normal. Although obsessions and compulsions may bring about a sense of relief and security in the short term, their cost is great. As much as obsessions and compulsions may bring about a sense of control, in the long run they only increase the extent to which you feel out of control. They can also greatly interfere with your ability to feel connected to others and build a meaningful and productive life. The skills we presented in this chapter may be your first step in overcoming your obsessions and compulsions and, in doing so, reclaiming your life. Keep in mind, however, that overcoming obsessions and compulsions can be a very difficult journey. Be patient and practice self-compassion, and at each moment along the way, make sure you recognize the progress you are making on this journey.

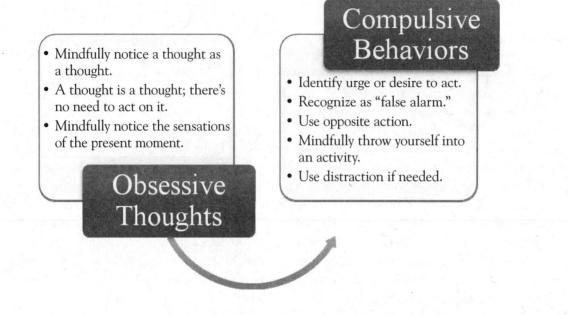

Figure 9.1   **Putting It All Together: DBT Skills to Manage Obsessions and Compulsions**

CHAPTER 10

Social Anxiety

Many people struggle with some form of social anxiety. In fact, social anxiety disorder (also called social phobia) is the most common anxiety disorder (Hofmann and Barlow 2002; Kessler et al. 1994). Social anxiety can take many forms. For example, some people might consider themselves a little shy. Others might experience anxiety only when speaking in front of large crowds or eating in front of other people. And still other people may fear any kind of social situation. Regardless, social anxiety can have a big impact on a person's life. Think about how many times you are in the presence of another person during the day. There are probably too many situations to count. It would be hard to live your life in such a way that you don't come into some kind of contact with another person. Therefore, having high levels of anxiety about being in social situations can greatly disrupt a person's life and cause considerable suffering.

SITUATIONS THAT CAN BRING ON SOCIAL ANXIETY

There are a number of different situations or activities that are considered "social." The most common situation that tends to bring on social anxiety is public speaking (Hofmann and Barlow 2002). Other types of situations that may lead to social anxiety are eating or writing in front of other people, holding a conversation with someone, being assertive, and using a crowded public restroom. The list could go on and on. People with social anxiety may be able to do many of these things without any concern or hesitation when they are alone. When these behaviors need to be done in front of another person (or a whole group of people), however, someone with social anxiety will probably experience a lot of anxiety and fear. Sometimes, this anxiety can be so great that the person has a panic attack. Basically, social anxiety results from any type of situation or activity where there is the potential to be seen and evaluated by others.

Now, the type of situations that bring on social anxiety can differ from person to person. In fact, some mental health professionals have suggested that all social anxiety can be organized into one of three different categories: generalized, nongeneralized, and circumscribed (Heimberg et al. 1993). Some people experience anxiety only in one type of social situation, such as public speaking. Because they don't have anxiety in other types of situations, this is considered *circumscribed social anxiety*, or social anxiety that is isolated to one type of situation. In *nongeneralized social anxiety*, a person might experience anxiety in a number of different social situations but feel comfortable in at least one type of social situation (for example, chatting informally with another person). In *generalized social anxiety*, a person experiences anxiety in social situations regardless of the type of social situation. The following exercise can help you identify the types of social situations that bring up anxiety for you.

Exercise 10.1 What Types of Situations Make You Anxious?

Mark all that apply.

	Public speaking
	Eating in front of other people
	Writing in front of another person
	Meeting new people
	Being in large crowds of people
	Using a public restroom
	Being assertive
	Talking to a member of the opposite sex
	Going to a social gathering (such as a party)
	Talking with superiors or people in authority positions (such as your boss or a professor)
	Making a telephone call in public
	Taking a test
	Having to return something to a store
	Changing or correcting an order at a restaurant
	Disagreeing with someone
	Calling someone you don't know very well

Are there other social situations that make you anxious? List them.
1.
2.
3.
4.
5.
6.
7.

WHAT DRIVES SOCIAL ANXIETY?

Researchers are still studying all of the different causes of social anxiety, but one thing is quite clear: fears of being evaluated by others seem to be at the core of social anxiety. Now, many people with social anxiety fear that other people will evaluate them negatively during social situations. More specifically, people with social anxiety often fear that something they do or say will cause others to evaluate them negatively (Schultz and Heimberg 2008). And who wouldn't be at least somewhat anxious about this prospect? Negative evaluation isn't something that many people look forward to. In fact, the link between possible negative evaluation and anxiety makes so much sense that there was a time when researchers thought that it was the fear of negative evaluation in particular that was at the center of social anxiety (Rapee and Heimberg 1997). Recently, though, researchers have begun to wonder about the importance of positive evaluation as well.

There is reason to believe that people with social anxiety may fear positive evaluation in addition to negative evaluation (Weeks et al. 2008). On the surface, this may not seem to make much sense. It feels good when others see us in a positive light, right? Well, not always. Being evaluated positively can make people feel that the bar has been raised and they will therefore need to meet higher standards in the future. If they also believe that it won't be possible to meet these higher standards, either because they think their good performance was just a fluke or because they believe they just can't do any better, they will probably experience anxiety (Wallace and Alden 1997). Receiving positive evaluation can also make people feel that they are now in the spotlight, resulting in an even greater chance that other people will be watching and evaluating them (Weeks, Jakatdar, and Heimberg 2010).

CONSEQUENCES OF FEARING EVALUATION

Fearing evaluation by others and the social anxiety you may experience as a result can have a tremendous influence on your life. As we will discuss in more detail later, these fears can interfere with your effectiveness in certain situations (for example, at work or school), your ability to form close relationships with other people, and your self-esteem. The good news is that there are a number of DBT skills that can help address many of the negative consequences of fearing evaluation. Next, we describe several common consequences of fearing evaluation and the specific DBT skills that can help you with these symptoms. If you experience other symptoms as a result of being in social situations (for example, panic attacks or worry), make sure to check out the chapters specifically devoted to these symptoms; you will find the DBT skills in those chapters helpful for dealing with these additional symptoms of social anxiety.

Self-Focused Attention

Many people with social anxiety believe that others have high standards for their behavior and that they will not be able to meet these standards. Consequently, when they find themselves in a social situation, they often focus most (if not all) of their attention on their own behavior and performance, with the goal of making sure that they perform as well as they can. Now, in some ways this makes a lot of sense. If you want to do well in a situation, it can be helpful to pay attention to what you are doing and to really focus your attention on your behavior. The problem is that this level of self-focused attention can backfire, especially when you are bound to experience anxiety. Think about it this way: because people with social anxiety often go into social situations believing that they will never be able to meet the standards of their audience (whether it is a large crowd or just one person), they often experience many symptoms of anxiety in these situations, including increased heart rate, blushing, sweating, and shaking. Now, just having these symptoms is not a problem in and of itself; everyone gets nervous at times, and most of the time other people probably don't even notice (or care). When you are focusing all of your attention on yourself and your behavior, however, these types of symptoms are bound to capture your attention and verify your belief that you are not meeting the standards of your audience. And, as you can probably guess, this just further increases your anxiety, contributing to a vicious cycle of negative evaluation of your own performance and growing anxiety (Clark and Wells 1995).

If you struggle with social anxiety, you are probably well aware of the downside of focusing too much attention on yourself and how difficult it can be to break this cycle once you get caught up in it. That's where some of the DBT skills can help.

REDIRECTING YOUR ATTENTION OUTWARD

One way that DBT skills can help you break this vicious cycle of self-focused attention and increasing anxiety is by preventing the cycle from developing to begin with. And the best way to do this is to redirect your attention toward your external environment. If you are experiencing a high level of anxiety as a result of how you think you appear to others, your attention is bound to be drawn to these very symptoms of anxiety, and you will probably have a great deal of difficulty focusing your attention on anything else. The DBT mindfulness skills of noticing and labeling your experience (Linehan 1993b) can help you focus your attention outward on your external environment. Rather than focusing all of your attention on your own behaviors and symptoms of anxiety, use these skills to help you get in touch with everything that is going on around you. Notice all aspects of your external environment, focusing on small details that you often over-look. Next, see if you can describe your environment in as much detail as possible. What do you see in front of you? What colors, textures, and shapes do you observe? What textures or sensations do you feel against your skin? Focus your attention on describing your environment as objectively as possible.

If you find yourself getting distracted by your internal experiences or once again focusing your attention on your symptoms of anxiety, use the DBT skill of focusing attention on one thing at a time (Linehan 1993b) to help you refocus your attention on your external environment. Focus all of your attention on just the world around you, throwing yourself into noticing and labeling your external environment and concentrating your mind only on that. If you find yourself getting distracted by your symptoms of anxiety, notice that, and then gently bring your mind back to what you notice outside of yourself and your body. Do this as many times as you need to, refocusing your attention again and again.

NOTICING YOUR INTERNAL EXPERIENCES WITHOUT JUDGMENT

In addition to helping you focus your attention on something other than yourself and your internal experiences, DBT mindfulness skills can also help address some of the negative consequences of self-focused attention. Specifically, you can use the DBT skill of noticing your experience without judgment (Linehan 1993b) to help break the cycle of self-directed attention that leads to even more anxiety. Indeed, although focusing all of your attention on your internal experiences and symptoms of anxiety will often just further increase your anxiety, this doesn't have to be the case. Instead, the reason why this form of self-directed attention often backfires is because so many people judge or evaluate their anxiety symptoms. Noticing that your heart is racing or your hands are shaking doesn't have to make you feel worse. It doesn't have to cause you problems. The problem is that most people end up judging their anxiety symptoms. Instead of just noticing their shortness of breath, they judge themselves and think that this is a sign of weakness or failure. Instead of noticing a racing heart, they evaluate this as negative or catastrophic. These evaluations, which often go hand in hand with observations of anxiety symptoms, cause problems. Just noticing these symptoms, in and of itself, will not hurt you.

So, when you notice your anxiety and the bodily sensations that accompany it, make sure to take a nonevaluative stance. Allow yourself to notice these experiences without judging or evaluating them. Focus on just noticing and labeling each aspect of your experience as it is, rather than judging it as bad, weak, pathetic, or wrong. Keep in mind that anxiety and all of the sensations that go along with it are simply a natural part of being alive and are something that every human being experiences. Observing your internal experiences in this way will help you connect with the fact that your symptoms of anxiety are not problematic in and of themselves. And this will go a long way in helping you break the cycle of self-focused attention leading to more anxiety, leading to even more self-focused attention, and so on. Review exercise 8.6 for some simple step-by-step instructions for noticing your anxiety and the bodily sensations that accompany this anxiety without judgment or evaluation.

Attention to Potential Signs of Negative Evaluation in Your Environment

Now, as much as learning how to redirect your attention toward your external environment will probably help with some of the problems that go along with focusing all of your attention on yourself and your internal experiences, this might not be enough. You see, studies have found that people with social anxiety are more likely to notice and direct their attention toward things in their environments that are threatening or suggest that their fears may be true (Schultz and Heimberg 2008).

For example, let's say that you are giving a talk in front of a large audience. If you experience social anxiety, your attention is probably going to be captured by the one person in the audience who is frowning, even if there are a number of other people who are smiling and giving you positive feedback. In addition, once your attention latches onto that person frowning, it will be difficult to redirect your attention away from that person's face. What's more, even though the person could be frowning about a number of different things (maybe from hunger or just a bad day), there's a really good chance that once your attention is focused on this frown, you will interpret it as a sign that you are not performing well, leading to even more anxiety and further increasing your attention to anything negative in your environment. Therefore, in addition to focusing your attention on your external environment, it's important to remember to expand your awareness to include all aspects of your environment. If you find that you are focusing on only one person or aspect of your environment, practice expanding your attention to take in all of the information around you, focusing on everything you notice. Doing so will help you connect with a more balanced evaluation of your performance.

This is also another time when noticing your experience without judgment or evaluation can be helpful. Rather than judging what you observe in your environment, focus on simply noticing it as it is and describing it objectively, letting go of any evaluations (Linehan 1993b). Now, you may notice that these evaluations continue to pop into your head from time to time, especially when you first start practicing this skill. This is natural and to be expected. If this happens, simply notice this evaluation or judgmental thought and return your attention to noticing and describing the things around you. The goal is to not completely eliminate judgments and evaluations (which would be impossible), but to change how you respond to these types of thoughts so that you don't get caught up in them as much.

Once your eyes are wide open and you are noticing all aspects (or as many as you can) of your environment without judgment, it can also help tremendously to really throw yourself into, or immerse yourself in, whatever activity you are doing right now, in the present moment. If you are speaking in front of an audience, really throw your whole mind and body into the activity, making it the single most important activity in the universe right now. In fact, you can always do this, no matter what you are doing, and it will almost always help.

Avoidance of Social Situations

One major way in which social anxiety can interfere with a person's life is by leading to avoidance. If you experience intense anxiety in social situations, it makes a lot of sense that you might want to limit that anxiety by staying away from those types of situations. As mentioned, though, it is practically impossible to avoid all social situations, and attempting to do so will severely limit your life. Trying to avoid social situations that lead to anxiety will likely interfere with establishing close relationships or developing new relationships. It will also have an impact on the types of jobs you can do, because so many jobs involve talking in front of other people or being evaluated by others. Finally, trying to avoid social situations could simply limit the activities available to you in your everyday life, because so many involve being around other people. In all of these ways, although the desire to avoid the situations that bring about anxiety is understandable, acting on this desire probably won't work in the long run and will probably just add to your distress. Therefore, a big part of overcoming social anxiety is to break down the avoidance it causes, and the DBT skill of acting opposite to your fear can help with this (Linehan 1993b).

APPROACHING FEARED SOCIAL SITUATIONS

As we discussed in chapter 8, avoiding the things you fear, when these things are not actually dangerous or threatening, will only exacerbate your fear. If the social situations feared by people with social anxiety were truly dangerous or life threatening, we would teach you skills to avoid them, in much the same way we teach children not to get into cars with strangers. With social anxiety, however, people come to fear all kinds of social situations that are not inherently dangerous. And, because they then avoid these situations, their fear continues and may intensify. Therefore, just as we discussed in the case of panic attacks and PTSD symptoms, the way to conquer this fear and keep social anxiety from hurting your life is to approach the situations you have been avoiding.

To begin to apply this skill to social anxiety, use the following exercise to identify all of the social situations you have been avoiding in your life. Remember that these situations can vary in terms of the number of people who are actually present, ranging from one to two people to large crowds. You may find it helpful to refer back to exercise 10.1 to help you identify all of the situations you have been avoiding. Write down these situations in the first column.

Next, try to come up with some small, doable steps you can take to begin to approach these situations. What can you do to put yourself in these situations? Think about all of the things you can do to get yourself in contact with these situations and the small steps you can take to act opposite to your fear. For example, if you are afraid of eating in front of other people, perhaps you can start by chewing some gum in front of your best friend or snacking on some peanuts as you walk down the street. You don't need to begin by having a five-course dinner in front of a new date. All you need to do is start breaking down your avoidance of these activities one step at a time. Write down the steps you come up with in the second column.

Exercise 10.2 Beginning to Approach Feared Social Situations

Write down all of the social situations you have been avoiding out of fear of being evaluated.	Write down up to five steps you can take to begin to approach this situation. Focus on small, doable actions.
	1. 2. 3. 4. 5.
	1. 2. 3. 4. 5.
	1. 2. 3. 4. 5.
	1. 2. 3. 4. 5.
	1. 2. 3. 4. 5.

	1. 2. 3. 4. 5.
	1. 2. 3. 4. 5.
	1. 2. 3. 4. 5.
	1. 2. 3. 4. 5.
	1. 2. 3. 4. 5.
	1. 2. 3. 4. 5.

Nice work! As we discuss throughout this book, just identifying the steps you can take to begin to break the cycle of avoidance in anxiety disorders is a huge first step in overcoming the hold anxiety can have on your life. Just thinking about approaching these situations can be extremely anxiety provoking, so taking the time to identify all of the things you can do to begin to get into contact with these situations is an important step on your road to recovery. The next step is to begin to make your way through this list, doing one thing at a time to approach these situations and conquer your fear.

Use skills for tolerating anxiety. Now, we realize that approaching the situations that scare you the most is probably easier said than done. Even if you understand the principles behind the skill of acting opposite to your fear and know on an intellectual level that avoiding these situations will only make your anxiety worse, it may still be incredibly difficult to bring yourself to approach them. And if you do begin to take steps to approach these situations, you will likely experience a lot of anxiety. Therefore, as you begin to approach your feared social situations, it can be useful to combine the skill of acting opposite to your fear with other DBT skills focused on helping you tolerate anxiety.

One of the most useful skills for tolerating anxiety is actually a simple one: breathing (Linehan 1993b). And, yet, just because this skill is simple does not mean it is easy to do. Surprisingly enough, most people in this world don't actually know how to breathe correctly, and a lot of people breathe in a way that can actually increase their anxiety. So, one basic skill for managing anxiety is simply to learn how to breathe properly. And this means learning how to use your *diaphragm* (the big muscle between your lungs and your stomach) to breathe.

So, how do you know if you're breathing properly? Take a few minutes to breathe in and out slowly. As you breathe, notice the parts of your body that move in and out or up and down with each breath. If you are breathing properly, your belly should push out when you breathe in and go back in when you breathe out. If your belly expands and contracts as you breathe, you are using your diaphragm to breathe. If, on the other hand, your shoulders move up and down as you breathe, you are probably not breathing properly, and you may be putting yourself at risk for more anxiety.

Training yourself to use your diaphragm to breathe will help you take deeper breaths, and taking deeper breaths means breathing slower. Deep, slow breathing is the body's natural way of combating anxiety. In fact, breathing out slowly can actually slow down your heart rate when you are anxious. Therefore, deep breathing is one of the most basic strategies for tolerating anxiety. The following exercise, adapted from our book *Freedom from Self-Harm* (Gratz and Chapman 2009), provides some simple step-by-step instructions for learning how to breathe deeply. Try it and see how it works!

Exercise 10.3 Learn How to Breathe Deeply

When you first practice this exercise, try to do it at a time when you already feel relaxed. It's easier to learn the basic techniques of deep breathing when you're not stressed out.

1. Find a comfortable and quiet place to practice your breathing. Sit up in a chair so that your back is straight and supported.

2. Close your eyes.

3. Put the palm of one of your hands on your stomach and the other on your chest across your breastbone.

4. Breathe in and out as you normally do. Which hand moves the most when you breathe? The one on your belly or the one on your chest? If the hand on your chest moves and the one on your belly doesn't, this means that you're not breathing with your diaphragm.

5. Now, when you breathe in and out, deliberately push out your belly when you breathe in, and let your belly fall when you breathe out. It may feel slightly unnatural at first. This is normal, and this feeling will go away very quickly with practice.

6. Continue to breathe in and out. Try to lengthen your breaths. Slowly count to five as you breathe in, and again when you breathe out. Also, try to breathe in through your nose and exhale through your mouth. This may help you take deeper breaths.

7. Practice this breathing exercise a couple of times a day. The more you practice, the more it will become a habit.

Once you've practiced this exercise a few times and are more familiar with deep breathing, try it when you feel anxious. Even though it may seem simple, changing your breathing can have a profound effect on your anxiety.

Another skill that can help you tolerate the anxiety you will probably feel when you start approaching social situations is progressive muscle relaxation (PMR), introduced earlier in this book, which involves tensing and then relaxing all of the various muscles in your body. This skill is one of the best around for reducing anxiety and promoting relaxation. Follow these steps, adapted from our book *Freedom from Self-Harm* (Gratz and Chapman 2009), to begin to practice PMR.

Exercise 10.4 Simple Steps for Practicing Progressive Muscle Relaxation

Follow these steps to practice PMR.

1. Find a quiet place where you won't be disturbed, and get into a comfortable position. You can do this lying down, sitting up, or even standing up, but you might find that it works best if you're lying down.

2. Find a place on your body to start the exercise. Many people find it helpful to start with the top of the head or the tips of their toes.

3. Bring your full attention to that part of your body. Let's say that you've started with your forearms. Imagine that your whole focus is being drawn down to your forearms. Then, clench your hands into fists, squeeze to about 75 to 80 percent of your maximum strength, and hold this tension for about five to ten seconds.

4. Let go and relax your muscles. Notice the difference between how they felt when they were tense and how they feel now. Just notice any sensations of relaxation or warmth, or anything else you might experience.

5. Repeat that process, first tensing the same muscles, holding that tension for five to ten seconds, and then relaxing those muscles.

6. Move to another area of your body. For instance, you might try your lower legs. Focus your attention on your calf muscles, and really try to clench them. Hold for five to ten seconds again, and then let go, relaxing your calves. Repeat this process to really relax those muscles.

7. Continue going through different muscle groups in your body, doing exactly the same thing. Each time, just tense your muscles about 75 to 80 percent for about five to ten seconds, and then relax them, focusing on the difference you feel.

Do PMR for five to twenty-five minutes, depending on how much time you have. Even doing it for five minutes can make a difference. So, try it out and see how much better you feel!

Not Getting Your Needs Met in Social Situations

As mentioned, even if you try to avoid most social situations, avoiding them completely just isn't possible. Therefore, people with social anxiety often try to find other ways of limiting the intense anxiety that can come from unavoidable social interactions. One of the most common ways is to try to limit the chances of negative evaluation by avoiding any kind of conflict (or even the possibility of conflict). For example, many people with social anxiety try not to stand out in social situations. They may avoid eye contact, speak softly, or not express their needs (Hofmann, Heinrichs, and Moscovitch 2004). And, if your goal is to avoid any kind of conflict or negative evaluation, these kinds of behaviors make a lot of sense. Think about how these behaviors likely influence social interactions. Acting in this way in a social situation probably makes it less likely that others will notice you. These behaviors also probably decrease the chance that you'll say something that upsets or offends someone else (which could result in negative evaluation). In addition, these types of behaviors also limit the chance of positive evaluation by others, which, as we discussed, can also be threatening to someone with social anxiety.

Of course, a major downside of this approach to social situations is that you probably won't get your needs met in these interactions. You may begin to feel like a doormat and as if you are not being taken seriously. These behaviors can also strengthen the idea that you aren't capable of successfully managing social interactions, reducing your self-respect and self-esteem. The good news, though, is that as scary as it may be to think about being more assertive in social situations, there are some really useful DBT skills that focus on helping people get their needs met and maintain their self-respect while also maintaining good relationships with others. And, this is a really important point: being assertive and asking for what you need in relationships does not mean that you need to sacrifice those relationships or walk around upsetting everyone in your life. This is a common misconception. Instead, there is a whole set of DBT interpersonal effectiveness skills focused on helping you learn to balance getting your needs met, maintaining strong relationships, and keeping your self-respect (Linehan 1993b) so that you don't have to sacrifice any of them.

GETTING WHAT YOU WANT OUT OF YOUR INTERACTIONS

So, how does this set of skills work? Well, the first step is to figure out what you want out of the interaction (Linehan 1993b). What are your goals? What are you trying to achieve? Do you want to say no to a request or get something specific from someone else? The first step is to figure out what you want.

Next, develop a script for stating your needs and asking for what you want. Begin by explaining the situation as clearly as possible. Make sure to describe it objectively. Next, let the person know how you feel about the situation using "I feel" and "I think" statements. This is the time when you can explain your opinions about the situation and where you are coming from. Then, state your needs and what you want out of the situation. Be as specific as possible and directly state what it is that you want the person to do. Finally, explain how doing what you ask or giving you what you need will benefit the other person. This is a step that is not always found in basic assertiveness training, but we believe it is incredibly important. Basically, the goal of this final step is to make it clear to the other person up front that there are benefits to doing what you ask and that giving you what you need can be a win-win situation (or at least can help the other person in some important ways). See the *Skills Training Manual for Treating Borderline Personality Disorder* (Linehan 1993b) for more specifics on these skills.

Now, as you probably know by now, getting your needs met is usually not as simple as just asking for what you want. Often, other people may not be able or willing to give you everything you ask for, no matter how skillfully you ask! Therefore, once you have figured out what it is you want and how to go about asking for it, there is one more step you need to take to prepare for this interaction. Specifically, you need to think about the compromises you are willing to make if the other person cannot or will not give you everything you are asking for. Thinking this through ahead of time is really important. It can be hard to think on your feet and consider all of the consequences of various options when you are in the middle of an interaction and experiencing anxiety. So, do your homework and identify the compromises that are and are not acceptable to you. This will go a long way in making the interaction go as smoothly as possible if you encounter any roadblocks. Exercise 10.5 walks you through the process of getting your needs met step by step. Use this exercise to plan for an upcoming interaction.

Exercise 10.5 Steps for Getting Your Needs Met in Interpersonal Interactions

1. Clarify your goals for the interactions. Ask yourself the following:

    What do I want out of this interaction? What are my goals for this interaction?

2. Develop a script for stating your needs and describing what you want. Be sure to complete all of the following sections.

    Explain the situation:

    Let the person know how you feel about the situation, using "I feel" and "I think" statements:

    State your needs and what you want out of the situation. Be as specific as possible:

    Clarify up front how this will benefit the other person. Explain why giving you what you need or accepting your request will make things better for the other person:

    Identify compromises you are willing to make. Make sure that you have thought about this ahead of time. Even if you don't have to offer a compromise, it is good to know how much you are willing to bend or give to reach an agreement. Write down the compromises you are willing to make here:

3. Practice this script until you feel comfortable with it. Practice as many times as you need to. Try it out in front of a mirror, or with a close friend or loved one. Focus on your nonverbal behaviors (tone of voice, facial expressions) in addition to the words you are saying.

4. When you feel prepared (which does not mean you won't feel anxious), approach the other person and ask for what you want. Keep in mind that this skill (just like all of the others we have taught you) gets easier with practice. The more you practice asking for what you want in relationships, the more comfortable you will become and the more likely you will be to get some of your needs met! You may also want to pair this skill with some of the skills we taught you for tolerating anxiety, including deep breathing and PMR.

Balance your needs with those of your relationships. In the same way that the DBT mindfulness skills we described earlier specify not just what to do but how to do it, the DBT interpersonal effectiveness skills also focus a lot on how to say the things you are going to say and the most effective way of delivering your request (Linehan 1993b). The following are pointers to keep in mind when asking for what you want or need in a relationship.

- Always keep the purpose of the interaction in mind; don't bring up other issues or allow yourself to be distracted. It can be really easy when discussing concerns you have about someone's behavior to fall into the trap of bringing up other relationship issues or other things you are upset about. As much as possible, try not to do this. Instead, keep the purpose of the particular interaction at hand in mind and try to stick to just that topic. This will probably be far more effective than bringing up other issues or conflicts from the past.

- Express yourself clearly, using a calm, confident tone. Focus on keeping your voice at a normal volume, refraining from raising your voice or speaking too softly. Focus on having a relaxed posture and facial expression. This will help you feel more relaxed. Make sure to maintain eye contact when you are speaking.

- Be respectful of the person with whom you are interacting. Listen to the person's response and validate her or his perspective and feelings on the issue. Even if you disagree with the person, respect the validity of her or his position.

- Be direct and genuine in the interaction. State your position clearly and honestly, and do not lie or make up excuses. Be true to your point of view and the validity of your request.

We realize that being assertive in relationships can seem like a very daunting task. Even for people without social anxiety, negotiating relationships is hard work and can be a stressful experience. In the end, though, expressing your needs and asserting yourself will only make your relationships stronger and more fulfilling. And, just as with all of the other skills we have taught you, the more you practice these skills, the easier they will become and the more comfortable you will get with them. So, think about what you want out of some upcoming interactions and use the previous steps to help you get your needs met. Remember, you deserve this!

MOVING FORWARD

In this chapter, we presented a lot of information on social anxiety and the different skills that may be useful in overcoming it. Remember, gaining more comfort and confidence in social situations is a process. There may be times when you are really pleased with how you did in a social situation and other times when you don't think things went as well. That is to be expected. Unfortunately, no one can control how other people respond. This means that there will be times when people give you negative feedback regardless of whether or not you deserve it. The most important thing is that you do the best you can in social situations and recognize that you are human. So, make sure to approach yourself with compassion and acceptance as you practice these skills, and you will find that you are well on your way to overcoming your social anxiety.

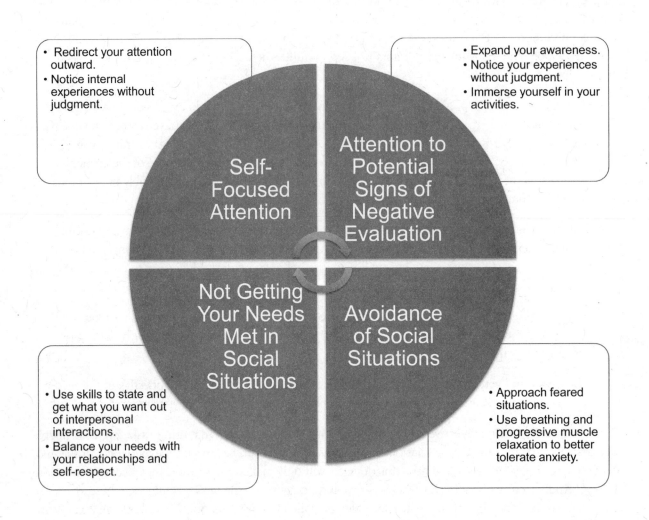

Figure 10.1   **Putting It All Together: DBT Skills to Manage Difficulties with Social Anxiety**

References

Agaibi, C. E., and J. P. Wilson. 2005. "Trauma, PTSD, and Resilience: A Review of the Literature." *Trauma, Violence, and Abuse* 6 (3):195–216.

American Psychiatric Association (APA). 2000. *Diagnostic and Statistical Manual of Mental Disorders (DSM-IV-TR)*. 4th ed. Text rev. Arlington, VA: American Psychiatric Association.

Baer, L. 2000. *Getting Control: Overcoming Your Obsessions and Compulsions*. Rev. ed. New York: Plume.

Baer, R. A. 2003. "Mindfulness Training as a Clinical Intervention: A Conceptual and Empirical Review." *Clinical Psychology: Science and Practice* 10 (2):125–43.

Barlow, D. H. 2002a. "The Nature of Anxious Apprehension." In *Anxiety and Its Disorders: The Nature and Treatment of Anxiety and Panic*, 2nd ed., edited by D. H. Barlow, 64–104. New York: The Guilford Press.

———. 2002b. "The Origins of Anxious Apprehension, Anxiety Disorders, and Related Emotional Disorders: Triple Vulnerabilities." In *Anxiety and Its Disorders: The Nature and Treatment of Anxiety and Panic*, 2nd ed., edited by D. H. Barlow, 252–91. New York: The Guilford Press.

———. 2002c. "The Phenomenon of Panic." In *Anxiety and Its Disorders: The Nature and Treatment of Anxiety and Panic*, 2nd ed., edited by D. H. Barlow, 105–38. New York: The Guilford Press.

Barlow, D. H., L. B. Allen, and M. L. Choate. 2004. "Toward a Unified Treatment for Emotional Disorders." *Behavior Therapy* 35 (2):205–30.

Barlow, D. H., B. F. Chorpita, and J. Turovsky. 1996. "Fear, Panic, Anxiety, and Disorders of Emotion." In *Perspectives on Anxiety, Panic, and Fear: Volume 43 of the Nebraska Symposium on Motivation*, edited by D. A. Hope, 251–328. Lincoln, NE: University of Nebraska Press.

Beck, A. T. 1995. "Cognitive Therapy: Past, Present, and Future." In *Cognitive and Constructive Psychotherapies: Theory, Research, and Practice*, edited by M. J. Mahoney, 29–40. New York: Springer Publishing Company.

Beck, J. G., D. M. Grant, J. D. Clapp, and S. A. Palyo. 2009. "Understanding the Interpersonal Impact of Trauma: Contributions of PTSD and Depression." *Journal of Anxiety Disorders* 23 (4):443–50.

Berle, D., and V. Starcevic. 2005. "Thought-Action Fusion: Review of the Literature and Future Directions." *Clinical Psychology Review* 25 (3):263–84.

Borkovec, T. D. 1985. "The Role of Cognitive and Somatic Cues in Anxiety and Anxiety Disorders: Worry and Relaxation-Induced Anxiety." In *Anxiety and the Anxiety Disorders*, edited by A. Tuma and J. D. Maser, 463–78. Hillsdale, NJ: Lawrence Erlbaum Associates.

Borkovec, T. D., O. M. Alcaine, and E. Behar. 2004. "Avoidance Theory of Worry and Generalized Anxiety Disorder." In *Generalized Anxiety Disorder: Advances in Research and Practice*, edited by R. G. Heimberg, C. L. Turk, and D. S. Mennin, 77–108. New York: The Guilford Press.

Borkovec, T. D., and L. Roemer. 1995. "Perceived Functions of Worry among Generalized Anxiety Disorder Subjects: Distraction from More Emotionally Distressing Topics?" *Journal of Behavior Therapy and Experimental Psychiatry* 26 (1):25–30.

Bouton, M. E., S. Mineka, and D. H. Barlow. 2001. "A Modern Learning Theory Perspective on the Etiology of Panic Disorder." *Psychological Review* 108 (1):4–32.

Bowen, S., N. Chawla, and G. A. Marlatt. 2011. *Mindfulness-Based Relapse Prevention for Addictive Behaviors: A Clinician's Guide*. New York: The Guilford Press.

Brewerton, T. D., R. B. Lydiard, D. B. Herzog, A. W. Brotman, P. M. O'Neil, and J. C. Ballenger. 1995. "Comorbidity of Axis I Psychiatric Disorders in Bulimia Nervosa." *Journal of Clinical Psychiatry* 56 (2):77–80.

Brown, T. A., and D. H. Barlow. 2002. "Classification of Anxiety and Mood Disorders." In *Anxiety and Its Disorders: The Nature and Treatment of Anxiety and Panic*, 2nd ed., edited by D. H. Barlow, 292–327. New York: The Guilford Press.

Brown, T. A., L. A. Campbell, C. L. Lehman, J. R. Grisham, and R. B. Mancill. 2001. "Current and Lifetime Comorbidity of the DSM-IV Anxiety and Mood Disorders in a Large Clinical Sample." *Journal of Abnormal Psychology* 110 (4):585–99.

Chapman, A. L., K. L. Gratz, and M. Z. Brown. 2006. "Solving the Puzzle of Deliberate Self-Harm: The Experiential Avoidance Model." *Behaviour Research and Therapy* 44 (3):371–94.

Chapman, A. L., and M. M. Linehan. 2005. "Dialectical Behavior Therapy for Borderline Personality Disorder." In *Borderline Personality Disorder*, edited by M. C. Zanarini, 211–42. Boca Raton, FL: Taylor & Francis.

Clark, D. M. 1988. "A Cognitive Model of Panic Attacks." In *Panic: Psychological Perspectives*, edited by S. Rachman and J. D. Maser, 71–89. Hillsdale, NJ: Lawrence Erlbaum Associates.

Clark, D. M., and A. Wells. 1995. "A Cognitive Model of Social Phobia." In *Social Phobia: Diagnosis, Assessment, and Treatment*, edited by R. G. Heimberg, M. R. Liebowitz, D. A. Hope, and F. R. Schneier, 69–93. New York: The Guilford Press.

Craske, M. G., and D. H. Barlow. 2008. "Panic Disorder and Agoraphobia." In *Clinical Handbook of Psychological Disorders: A Step-by-Step Treatment Manual*, 4th ed., edited by D. H. Barlow. New York: The Guilford Press.

Cromer, K. R., N. B. Schmidt, and D. L. Murphy. 2007. "An Investigation of Traumatic Life Events and Obsessive-Compulsive Disorder." *Behaviour Research and Therapy* 45 (7):1683–91.

Dorahy, M. J. 2010. "The Impact of Dissociation, Shame, and Guilt on Interpersonal Relationships in Chronically Traumatized Individuals: A Pilot Study." *Journal of Traumatic Stress* 23 (5):653–56.

Gailliot, M. T., and R. F. Baumeister. 2007. "The Physiology of Willpower: Linking Blood Glucose to Self-Control." *Personality and Social Psychology Review* 11 (4):303–27.

Godart, N. T., M. F. Flament, F. Curt, F. Perdereau, F. Lang, J. L. Venisse, et al. 2003. "Anxiety Disorders in Subjects Seeking Treatment for Eating Disorders: A DSM-IV Controlled Study." *Psychiatry Research* 117 (3):245–58.

Grant, B. F., D. S. Hasin, F. S. Stinson, D. A. Dawson, W. Ruan, R. B. Goldstein, S. M. Smith, T. D. Saha, and B. Huang. 2005. "Prevalence, Correlates, Co-Morbidity, and Comparative Disability of DSM-IV Generalized Anxiety Disorder in the USA: Results from the National Epidemiologic Survey on Alcohol and Related Conditions." *Psychological Medicine* 35 (12):1747–59.

Gratz, K. L., and A. L. Chapman. 2009. *Freedom from Self-Harm: Overcoming Self-Injury with Skills from DBT and Other Treatments*. Oakland, CA: New Harbinger Publications.

Gratz, K. L., M. T. Tull, and J. G. Gunderson. 2008. "Preliminary Data on the Relationship between Anxiety Sensitivity and Borderline Personality Disorder: The Role of Experiential Avoidance." *Journal of Psychiatric Research* 42 (7):550–59.

Gross, J. J. 1998. "The Emerging Field of Emotion Regulation: An Integrative Review." *Review of General Psychology* 2 (3):271–99.

Hayes, S. C., and S. Smith. 2005. *Get Out of Your Mind and Into Your Life: The New Acceptance and Commitment Therapy*. Oakland, CA: New Harbinger Publications.

Heimberg, R. G., C. S. Holt, F. R. Schneier, R. L. Spitzer, and M. R. Liebowitz. 1993. "The Issue of Subtypes in the Diagnosis of Social Phobia." *Journal of Anxiety Disorders* 7 (3):249–69.

Hofmann, S. G., and D. H. Barlow. 2002. "Social Phobia (Social Anxiety Disorder)." In *Anxiety and Its Disorders: The Nature and Treatment of Anxiety and Panic*, 2nd ed., edited by D. H. Barlow, 454–76. New York: The Guilford Press.

Hofmann, S. G., N. Heinrichs, and D. A. Moscovitch. 2004. "The Nature and Expression of Social Phobia: Toward a New Classification." *Clinical Psychology Review* 24 (7):769–97.

Kabat-Zinn, J. 1990. *Full Catastrophe Living: Using the Wisdom of Your Body and Mind to Face Stress, Pain, and Illness*. New York: Bantam Dell.

Keane, T. M., A. Marshall, and C. Taft. 2006. "Posttraumatic Stress Disorder: Etiology, Epidemiology, and Treatment Outcome." *Annual Review of Clinical Psychology*. 2:161-97.

Kessler, R. C., W. T. Chiu, R. Jin, A. M. Ruscio, K. Shear, and E. E. Walters. 2006. "The Epidemiology of Panic Attacks, Panic Disorder, and Agoraphobia in the National Comorbidity Survey Replication." *Archives of General Psychiatry* 63 (4):415–24.

Kessler, R. C., O. Demler, R. G. Frank, M. Olfson, H. A. Pincus, E. E. Walters, P. Wang, K. B. Wells, and A. M. Zaslavsky. 2005. "Prevalence and Treatment of Mental Disorders, 1990 to 2003." *New England Journal of Medicine* 352 (24):2515–23.

Kessler, R. C., K. A. McGonagle, S. Zhao, C. B. Nelson, M. Hughes, S. Eshleman, H. U. Wittchen, and K. S. Kendler. 1994. "Lifetime and 12-Month Prevalence of DSM-III-R Psychiatric Disorders in the United States: Results from the National Comorbidity Study." *Archives of General Psychiatry* 51 (1):8–19.

Kessler, R. C., C. B. Nelson, K. A. McGonagle, J. Liu, M. Swartz, and D. G. Blazer. 1996. "Comorbidity of DSM-III-R Major Depressive Disorder in the General Population: Results from the US National Comorbidity Survey." *British Journal of Psychiatry* 168 (Suppl. 30):17–30.

Kessler, R. C., A. Sonnega, E. Bromet, M. Hughes, and C. B. Nelson. 1995. "Posttraumatic Stress Disorder in the National Comorbidity Survey." *Archives of General Psychiatry* 52 (12):1048–60.

Klein, D. F. 1993. "Panic Disorder with Agoraphobia." *British Journal of Psychiatry* 163 (6):835–37.

LeDoux, J. 1996. *The Emotional Brain: The Mysterious Underpinnings of Emotional Life.* New York: Simon & Schuster.

Levin, R., and T. Nielsen. 2009. "Nightmares, Bad Dreams, and Emotion Dysregulation: A Review and New Neurocognitive Model of Dreaming." *Current Directions in Psychological Science* 18 (2):84–88.

Lieb, K., M. C. Zanarini, C. Schmahl, M. M. Linehan, and M. Bohus. 2004. "Borderline Personality Disorder." *Lancet* 364 (9432): 453–61.

Lindesay, J., S. Baillon, T. Brugha, M. Dennis, R. Stewart, R. Araya, and H. Meltzer. 2006. "Worry Content across the Lifespan: An Analysis of 16- to 74-Year-Old Participants in the British National Survey of Psychiatric Morbidity 2000." *Psychological Medicine* 36 (11):1625–33.

Linehan, M. M. 1993a. *Cognitive Behavioral Treatment of Borderline Personality Disorder.* New York: The Guilford Press.

———. 1993b. *Skills Training Manual for Treating Borderline Personality Disorder.* New York: The Guilford Press.

———. 2007. *Opposite Action: Changing Emotions You Want to Change—Dialectical Behavior Skills Training Video.* DVD. Directed by Behavioral Tech. New York: The Guilford Press.

MacLeod, C., A. Mathews, and P. Tata. 1986. "Attentional Bias in Emotional Disorders." *Journal of Abnormal Psychology* 95 (1):15–20.

McKay, M., J. C. Wood, J. Brantley, and T. Marra. 2007. *The Dialectical Behavior Therapy Skills Workbook: Practical DBT Exercises for Learning Mindfulness, Interpersonal Effectiveness, Emotional Regulation, and Distress Tolerance.* Oakland, CA: New Harbinger Publications.

McNally, R. J. 1994. *Panic Disorder: A Critical Analysis.* New York: The Guilford Press.

Mitte, K. 2008. "Trait-Disgust vs. Fear of Contamination and the Judgmental Bias of Contamination Concerns." *Journal of Behavior Therapy and Experimental Psychiatry* 39 (4):577–86.

Molina, S., T. D. Borkovec, C. Peasley, and D. Person. 1998. "Content Analysis of Worrisome Streams of Consciousness in Anxious and Dysphoric Participants." *Cognitive Therapy and Research* 22 (2):109–23.

Morissette, S. B., M. T. Tull, S. B. Gulliver, B. W. Kamholz, and R. T. Zimering. 2007. "Anxiety, Anxiety Disorders, Tobacco Use, and Nicotine: A Critical Review of Interrelationships." *Psychological Bulletin* 133 (2):245–72.

Novaco, R. W., and C. M. Chemtob. 1998. "Anger and Trauma: Conceptualization, Assessment, and Treatment." In *Cognitive-Behavioral Therapies for Trauma*, edited by V. M. Follette, J. I. Ruzek, and F. R. Abueg, 162–90. New York: The Guilford Press.

Orsillo, S. M., and L. Roemer. 2011. *The Mindful Way through Anxiety: Break Free from Chronic Worry and Reclaim Your Life.* New York: The Guilford Press.

Pallesen, S., I. H. Nordhus, G. H. Nielsen, O. E. Havik, G. Kvale, B. Johnsen, and S. Skjøtskift. 2001. "Prevalence of Insomnia in the Adult Norwegian Population." *Sleep* 24 (7):771–79.

Papp, L. A., D. F. Klein, and J. M. Gorman. 1993. "Carbon Dioxide Hypersensitivity, Hyperventilation, and Panic Disorder." *American Journal of Psychiatry* 150 (8):1149–57.

Rachman, S., and P. de Silva. 1978. "Abnormal and Normal Obsessions." *Behaviour Research and Therapy* 16 (4):233–48.

Radomsky, A. S., and S. Rachman. 2004. "Symmetry, Ordering, and Arranging Compulsive Behaviour." *Behaviour Research and Therapy* 42 (8):893–913.

Rapee, R. M., M. G. Craske, and D. H. Barlow. 1990. "Subject-Described Features of Panic Attacks Using Self-Monitoring." *Journal of Anxiety Disorders* 4 (2):171–81.

Rapee, R. M., and R. G. Heimberg. 1997. "A Cognitive-Behavioral Model of Anxiety in Social Phobia." *Behaviour Research and Therapy* 35 (8):741–56.

Reiss, S. 1991. "Expectancy Model of Fear, Anxiety, and Panic." *Clinical Psychology Review* 11 (2):141–53.

Robins, C. J., and A. L. Chapman. 2004. "Dialectical Behavior Therapy: Current Status, Recent Developments, and Future Directions." *Journal of Personality Disorders* 18 (1):73–79.

Robinson, J., J. Sareen, B. J. Cox, and J. Bolton. 2009. "Self-Medication of Anxiety Disorders with Alcohol and Drugs: Results from a Nationally Representative Sample." *Journal of Anxiety Disorders* 23 (1):38–45.

Roemer, L., S. Molina, and T. D. Borkovec. 1997. "An Investigation of Worry Content among Generally Anxious Individuals." *Journal of Nervous and Mental Disease* 185 (5):314–19.

Roemer, L., S. M. Orsillo, and D. H. Barlow. 2002. "Generalized Anxiety Disorder." In *Anxiety and Its Disorders: The Nature and Treatment of Anxiety and Panic*, 2nd ed., edited by D. H. Barlow, 477–515. New York: The Guilford Press.

Roemer, L., K. Salters, S. D. Raffa, and S. M. Orsillo. 2005. "Fear and Avoidance of Internal Experiences in GAD: Preliminary Tests of a Conceptual Model." *Cognitive Therapy and Research* 29 (1):71–88.

Sabourin, B. C., and S. H. Stewart. 2008. "Alcohol Use and Anxiety Disorders." In *Anxiety in Health Behaviors and Physical Illness*, edited by M. J. Zvolensky and J. A. J. Smits, 29–54. New York: Springer Science+Business Media.

Salkovskis, P. M., and J. Harrison. 1984. "Abnormal and Normal Obsessions: A Replication." *Behaviour Research and Therapy* 22 (5):549–52.

Salters-Pedneault, K., L. Roemer, M. T. Tull, L. Rucker, and D. S. Mennin. 2006. "Evidence of Broad Deficits in Emotion Regulation Associated with Chronic Worry and Generalized Anxiety Disorder." *Cognitive Therapy and Research* 30 (4):469–80.

Schmidt, N. B., M. J. Telch, and T. L. Jaimez. 1996. "Biological Challenge Manipulation of PCO_2 Levels: A Test of Klein's (1993) Suffocation Alarm Theory of Panic." *Journal of Abnormal Psychology* 105 (3):446–54.

Schmidt, N. B., and J. Trakowski. 2004. "Interoceptive Assessment and Exposure in Panic Disorder: A Descriptive Study." *Cognitive and Behavioral Practice* 11 (1):81–92.

Schultz, L. T., and R. G. Heimberg. 2008. "Attentional Focus in Social Anxiety Disorder: Potential for Interactive Processes." *Clinical Psychology Review* 28 (7):1206–21.

Shafran, R. 2002. "Eating Disorders and Obsessive Compulsive Disorder." In *Cognitive Approaches to Obsessions and Compulsions: Theory, Assessment, and Treatment*, edited by R. O. Frost and G. Steketee, 215–31. Amsterdam: Pergamon/Elsevier.

Soussignan, R. 2002. "Duchenne Smile, Emotional Experience, and Autonomic Reactivity: A Test of the Facial Feedback Hypothesis." *Emotion* 2 (1):52–74.

Spoormaker, V. I., and P. Montgomery. 2008. "Disturbed Sleep in Post-Traumatic Stress Disorder: Secondary Symptom or Core Feature?" *Sleep Medicine Reviews* 12 (3):169–84.

Stein, M. B., K. L. Jang, and W. J. Livesley. 1999. "Heritability of Anxiety Sensitivity: A Twin Study." *American Journal of Psychiatry* 156 (2):246–51.

Steketee, G. and D. H. Barlow. 2002. "Obsessive-Compulsive Disorder." In *Anxiety and Its Disorders: The Nature and Treatment of Anxiety and Panic*, 2nd ed., edited by D. H. Barlow, 516–50. New York: The Guilford Press.

Swinbourne, J. M., and S. W. Touyz. 2007. "The Co-Morbidity of Eating Disorders and Anxiety Disorders: A Review." *European Eating Disorders Review* 15 (4):253–74.

Swinson, R. P., C. Soulios, B. J. Cox, and K. Kuch. 1992. "Brief Treatment of Emergency Room Patients with Panic Attacks." *American Journal of Psychiatry* 149 (7):944–46.

Tallis, F., M. Eysenck, and A. Mathews. 1992. "A Questionnaire for the Measurement of Nonpathological Worry." *Personality and Individual Differences* 13 (2):161–68.

Tull, M. T., D. E. Baruch, M. S. Duplinsky, and C. W. Lejuez. 2008. "Illicit Drug Use across the Anxiety Disorders: Prevalence, Underlying Mechanisms, and Treatment." In *Anxiety in Health Behaviors and Physical Illness*, edited by M. J. Zvolensky and J. A. J. Smits, 55–79. New York: Springer Science+Business Media.

Tull, M. T., and L. Roemer. 2007. "Emotion Regulation Difficulties Associated with the Experience of Uncued Panic Attacks: Evidence of Experiential Avoidance, Emotional Nonacceptance, and Decreased Emotional Clarity." *Behavior Therapy* 38 (4):378–91.

Tull, M. T., A. Trotman, M. S. Duplinsky, E. K. Reynolds, S. B. Daughters, M. N. Potenza, and C. W. Lejuez. 2009. "The Effect of Post-Traumatic Stress Disorder on Risk-Taking Propensity among Crack/Cocaine Users in Residential Substance Abuse Treatment." *Depression and Anxiety* 26 (12):1158–64.

Wallace, S. T., and L. E. Alden. 1997. "Social Phobia and Positive Social Events: The Price of Success." *Journal of Abnormal Psychology* 106 (3):416–24.

Watt, M. C., and S. H. Stewart. 2000. "Anxiety Sensitivity Mediates the Relationships between Childhood Learning Experiences and Elevated Hypochondriacal Concerns in Young Adulthood." *Journal of Psychosomatic Research* 49 (2):107–18.

Weeks, J. W., R. G. Heimberg, T. L. Rodebaugh, and P. J. Norton. 2008. "Exploring the Relationship between Fear of Positive Evaluation and Social Anxiety." *Journal of Anxiety Disorders* 22 (3):386–400.

Weeks, J. W., T. A. Jakatdar, and R. G. Heimberg. 2010. "Comparing and Contrasting Fears of Positive and Negative Evaluation as Facets of Social Anxiety." *Journal of Social and Clinical Psychology* 29 (1):68–94.

Wegner, D. M., R. Erber, and S. Zanakos. 1993. "Ironic Processes in the Mental Control of Mood and Mood-Related Thought." *Journal of Personality and Social Psychology* 65 (6):1093–104.

Whiteside, U., E. Chen, C. Neighbors, D. Hunter, T. Lo, and M. Larimer. 2007. "Difficulties Regulating Emotions: Do Binge Eaters Have Fewer Strategies to Modulate and Tolerate Negative Affect?" *Eating Behaviors* 8 (2):162–69.

Zanarini, M. C., F. R. Frankenburg, E. D. Dubo, A. E. Sickel, A. Trikha, A. Levin, and V. Reynolds. 1998. "Axis I Comorbidity of Borderline Personality Disorder." *American Journal of Psychiatry* 155 (12):1733–39.

Alexander L. Chapman, PhD, is associate professor in the department of psychology at Simon Fraser University, a practicing registered psychologist, and president of the DBT Centre of Vancouver. He has published numerous articles and chapters on dialectical behavior therapy (DBT), trains professionals and students in DBT, and has coauthored books on behavior therapy, borderline personality disorder, and self-harm. In 2007, Chapman received a Young Investigator's Award from the National Education Alliance for Borderline Personality Disorder. In 2011, he received a Michael Smith Foundation for Health Research Award to support his work on borderline personality disorder, as well as a Canadian Psychological Association Early Career Scientist Practitioner Award for his work integrating research and treatment in DBT.

Kim L. Gratz, PhD, is associate professor in the department of psychiatry and human behavior at the University of Mississippi Medical Center, where she serves as director of the dialectical behavior therapy clinic and director of personality disorders research. In 2005, Gratz received a Young Investigator's Award from the National Education Alliance for Borderline Personality Disorder. She has written numerous journal articles and book chapters on borderline personality disorder, deliberate self-harm, and emotion regulation, and is coauthor of *The Borderline Personality Disorder Survival Guide* and *Freedom from Self-Harm*.

Matthew T. Tull, PhD, is associate professor and director of anxiety disorders research in the department of psychiatry and human behavior at the University of Mississippi Medical Center. He has published numerous articles and chapters on emotion regulation and anxiety disorders, with a particular emphasis on panic disorder, generalized anxiety disorder, and post-traumatic stress disorder. He received the Chaim and Bela Danieli Young Professional Award from the International Society for Traumatic Stress Studies in 2009, and the 2010 President's New Researcher Award from the Association for Behavioral and Cognitive Therapies for his research on post-traumatic stress disorder.

Foreword writer **Terence M. Keane, PhD**, is associate chief of staff for research and development and director of the behavioral sciences division of the National Center for PTSD at the VA Boston Healthcare System. He is also currently president of the Anxiety Disorders Association of America.

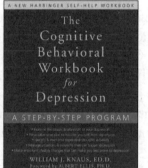